Empowering the Sensitive Male Soul

Highly Sensitive Men in Perspective

Tracy M. Cooper, Ph.D.

Invictus Publishing, llc

Empowering the Sensitive Male Soul

Highly Sensitive Men in Perspective

Edited by Kristina Martel

ISBN-9798632782876

Invictus Publishing, llc
2303 South 16th Street
Ozark, MO 65721

Author's website: www.drtracycooper.org

Printed by Kindle Direct Publishing
Printed in the United States of America
Published by Invictus Publishing, llc
First printing: 2020

Table of Contents

ACKNOWLEDGEMENTS

This book was made possible by the disparate bits and pieces that I picked up from different men, throughout my journey in life. From my father, who was inspiring in certain ways yet terrifying in others to my grandfather, who represented the wise sage in my youthful mind, to teachers who captivated me in various ways, to army drill sergeants who impressed upon me in not-so-subtle ways, *Moten Gators*. I absorbed these subtle, and, not so subtle, inferences regarding manhood and sought to embody something of an amalgamation of the best bits and pieces of each of my influences.

My father's passing when I was 15 left a massive, unresolved hole in my life that I have endeavored to reconcile all these decades later. Now, with two grown sons of my own, I enter the role of almost-elder sage. At 53, I have some ways to go yet, but in pausing to reflect on why I am the man I am now, it truly is a patchwork quilt of varying influences, coupled with my own choices in life, that have comprised my uniquc cxperience of life as a sensitive masculine soul.

It's been said, by Ram Dass, the great spiritual teacher, that we are all only "walking each other through this life" and I humbly acknowledge what each man who has passed through my life has gifted me. At times, I have only come to appreciate their gifts much later when I have matured to a greater degree myself. I also wish to acknowledge and recognize the many women who have contributed to who I am now and who I may become in the future. We truly cannot discuss masculinity without discussing femininity and appreciating that none of us exist in a vacuum.

In that regard, I wish to acknowledge my mother, Georgia (Lucy) Cooper, who has taught me compassion and patience; my wife, Lisa Cooper, who has been with me as an equal partner the entire journey; my grandmother, Gladys Vicie Cooper, who taught me to value family; my beloved late sister, Becky Smith, who passed from this world far too early, yet was so proud of her big brother and his accomplishments; Michele Mercer-Lee, my dear colleague and friend who provides her keen insights and views of my ongoing work, and the many other women who have passed through my life offering care, love, and support.

I would also like to acknowledge particular influential men in my life: my father, Claude Cooper, whose passing at the age of 49 haunted me through the years as I sought to better understand who he was and who I am; my grandfather, Claude Lee Cooper, who, once in talking to my mother about his son's kids said, while pointing at me "that boy's different, he's going to do something with his life," my brother, Tim Cooper, whom I was closest to growing up and led me on many adventures; my oldest brother, Claude Cooper Jr., who has become my dear brother again and added to the richness in my life the past few years; my little brother, Terry Cooper, whom I admire for his steadfast stability throughout life and good humor; my Army buddy Curt Schmidt, who knew me as a skinny 17 year old running to the military to escape Missouri and influenced me to see the value in higher education and to want it for myself, in time; and to the many wise sages who have become a part of my life, while guiding me, knowingly and unknowingly, I thank you and acknowledge your cumulative contributions to this masculine sensitive soul.

DEDICATION

For my sister, Rebecca Smith-Cooper, and my father, Claude Cooper, you both would have loved this book! For our dear Dr. Ted Zeff, who passed very peacefully in 2019, your unwavering dedication to raising consciousness in highly sensitive men has shown bright for 30+ years and made this work possible!

For my two sons, Peter Cooper and Benjamin Cooper and my two stepsons, Christopher Steward and Michael Steward. May this book help illuminate your paths forward in this world as men of resilience, courage, and kindness!

PREFACE

The rock singer Chris Cornell has just passed away at the age of 52 as I write this section and I am processing the loss of a tremendous talent of my generation while trying to understand how a man can commit suicide with two beautiful, young children and a wife he described as "a lioness, an angel...the perfect wife and mother." Do we expect too much of ourselves? Are we too stressed by the society we live in? Do men necessarily have to self-destruct, or can we live to grand old ages and play the role of sage to our younger counterparts? Chris Cornell, the lead singer for both Soundgarden and Audioslave, never appeared to be in crisis. Perhaps he suffered in silence like many of us do with depression, anxiety, and accumulated emotional baggage from our early lives that weighs us down like ticking time bombs waiting for the right moment to explode and take a part of us with it. Regardless of how we choose to view Cornell's death, masculinity carries with it a weight. That much is certain.

Writing this book, even just conceptualizing how to do it in a meaningful way has been very difficult. At times, I have been lost as to its ability to serve a purpose because the nature of masculinity seems to be so overwhelmingly negative, binary, and narrow in worldview. Where deep-thinking, deep-feeling men fit into this equation is a question I have pondered deeply. With Cornell's death so immediate at this moment, it is clear to me that our time in life is finite, and we must take necessary stands against the cultural mediocrity that has enveloped us. It is in our very ability to think and feel deeply, while processing critically and creatively, that we offer the world a broader vision of what is possible as men and what is possible for society.

I could have written this book in many ways but have chosen to mirror the research process I am familiar with, one that relies on input from multiple sources, along with my reasonable interpretations. As a transdisciplinary researcher, I draw on sociology, psychology, creativity studies, and other relevant fields to inform my research. I cannot offer ultimate solutions because the problem of masculinity is generational, culturally specific, and influenced deeply by personal choices related to power, privilege, and status. What seems to be a reasonable process to follow includes asking the questions: how did masculinity get to where it is at today? In what ways does it affect our lives (and the lives of others)? How can we redefine it in personal ways that might positively impact our lives and the larger culture? What are the implications for the future if we do? It is through this open-minded process of asking questions and seeking information to inform those questions that we may arrive at useful conceptualizations. I will ask you, along the way, to join me in considering viewpoints we might find challenging or foreign, but courage and curiosity will carry us far as we enter the web of complexity.

This book will not seek to provide simple, easy answers to complex problems. Instead, we will uncover ugly realities regarding our culture, and ourselves, and we will learn about their cost to us all. I believe there is a cathartic power in full-on exploration of issues that plague us in life. In a sense, we must act out the gestalt of masculinity rather than focus on hot-button issues. By confronting and carefully studying many aspects of masculinity, always with an open mind that acknowledges our inherent bias as beings of culture, we may achieve objectivity and see ourselves for what we are: human beings trying to navigate in a complex civilization that places multiple demands on us, typically not of our choosing.

Few of us are born knowing what life has in store for us. Most of us adapt and adjust to what life requires of us, sometimes sacrificing our bodies, our well-being, and our happiness. I do not contend that sacrifice is not necessary, but I do question *everything* because if we are to lead, we must know that our actions are worthwhile, that they do not harm others, and that they are the best actions for our families, communities, and societies. We have strayed far from action informed by concern for community and allowed individualism to pump up our egos, cast those not like us as "others," and to glorify unworthy aspects of humanity, such as violence and unbridled materialism to occupy a high status in our lives. We must put aside lower impulses and seek inward practices that can transform our lives and the lives of those around us. It is with empathy, cooperation, nurturing, and compassion, combined with goal setting and attainment, measured and moral actions, and benevolence that we may successfully navigate life's many vicissitudes while leaving the world a better place than we found it (while not harming others). In doing so, this nurtures our higher possible selves and fulfills the spiritual admonishing to "love thy brother as thyself."

Empowering the Sensitive Male Soul is not a book geared toward superficial bonding. Rather, it is a pragmatic look at masculinity for all people because masculinity does not exist in a vacuum. As men, we act out our masculinity, based on the expectations of others, how we think others perceive us, and on our cultural conditioning, which entails positive reinforcement for conforming behavior and negative sanctions for non-conforming behaviors. Here, we have an opportunity to truly think for ourselves, to cast off the non-thinking (or weak thinking) that typifies culture and to choose who we wish to be. This book is about celebrating highly sensitive males in all their glorious complexity, strength, and sheer potential!

FOREWORD

March 2020, while confined in my Manila condo high above the city's skyline, I came across an unexpected email requesting my contribution in Dr. Tracy Cooper's, "Empowering the Sensitive Male Soul" manuscript. I must admit I was surprised and inspired simultaneously, and I asked myself, why me? The only humble brag conclusion I could come up with was maybe it's because he knows I am honest, have uncompromising values, and share the same innate trait as a highly sensitive man (HSM).

I met Dr. Cooper while filming our first Sensitive documentary series "SENSITIVE - THE UNTOLD STORY" (STUS), the first documentary ever done on the trait. The film featured my mentor and International Best-Selling author Elaine Aron, Ph.D., who penned "The Highly Sensitive Person" and other volumes on the subject. Since then, I have directed "SENSITIVE AND IN LOVE" (SAIL) and "SENSITIVE LOVERS." (SL) When introduced to Dr. Cooper, I quickly concluded that he is a wordsmith and a poignant orator. I thought one day, this humble kind spirit would write a book that focused on the HSM. He has a way of crafting his words that reveal the HS MAN, as I have never observed. So, why me? Well, I guess we are like-minded! I appreciate the request and opportunity and will give it my best shot; this is not my forte.

I am a film director and blessed to have directed for Oprah Winfrey on her daytime talk show, ABC's Good Morning America and the Disney Channel, and more. These shows allowed me to sit across the table from many a kindred soul. People like Nelson Mandela (HSP), Prince Charles (HSP), Magic Johnson, Malcolm Forbes Sr. (HSP), and Dr. Seuss. All of these men I consider to be sensitive transformative leaders.

I must state that Dr. Cooper does not have his feet on the gas and the brake at the same time; he is in the fast lane. He moves to the point with fluidity, and I love it! For the past three years, I have been traveling around the world, conducting interviews with *Highly Sensitive Men* and non-highly sensitive men. I discovered that there is still that old, toxic masculinity lurking around the globe, holding many men back from authentic progress to finding their pure inner light. Many men I visited of Spanish, Italian, and German descent did *not* want us to interview them under the adage of 'Sensitivity.' I thought to myself it's 2020, *times they are a-changing'*. Dr. Cooper's unfathomable research and deep thinking have created a canvas to help men with fragile egos feel that it is ok not to be hard. Appropriately manifested, this trait will 'unleash' a unique gift in thousands of men around the world.

I come from a mixed family of predominately African American and Anglo-Saxon descent; it was not an easy childhood for me to traverse. My Father, the African American side of the equation, wanted me to be the *tough kid,* not *sensitive*, and fight my way through life rather than negotiate my way through existence. My Mother, bless her heart, was the opposite. Her life lesson taught me that I can express my sensitive emotions openly; that I do not have to be "tough all the time." My Father made it clear I would be thought of as "girlish" or weak. OMG! Thank God I took my mother's lead.

I am honored to voice this! I sincerely believe HS Men will be in GREAT demand for saving the world. Our candor, creativity, intelligence, empathy, profound thinking ability, and sensitive subtleties are a vast addition to the male ego. I say this with candid splendor as I, too, am a proud HS male.

Dr. Tracy Cooper's **Empowering the Sensitive Male Soul** is a blessing and a toolkit for those who need a few truthful words of wisdom that ensures *us* guys that it is TOTALLY cool to be Highly Sensitive. The best part of this volume is Tracy taking us under the hood of this tormenting subject as we discover what the scientists, the therapists, the Non-HSP's and the HSP's have to say about this innate trait in men. This concise and original body of work is on time and with the times.

Dr. Tracy Cooper's written words make everyone around him feel something.

Time's, they REALLY are a-changing! ~Will Harper

CHAPTER 1

Sensory Processing Sensitivity Explained

In this chapter, we will establish the core of research around Sensory Processing Sensitivity, then briefly examine the breadth of research that followed and continues today. With that firm foundation, grounded in the sciences, we will move forward and explore what it means to be a sensitive male soul.

Historical Basis: An Introduction

This book articulates its position through Sensory Processing Sensitivity: a multifaceted personality trait first identified and explicated in the mid-1990s by Drs. Arthur and Elaine Aron, working at Stony Brook University. As detailed in the 2015 documentary film, Sensitive-The Untold Story, Elaine Aron was engaged in therapy, as a patient, with a psychotherapist who suggested that she may be "highly sensitive," based on the way she described her sensitivities, overstimulation tendency, and anxieties.

Dr. Aron, who is a clinical psychologist and was a professor, at that time, along with her husband, also a psychologist and professor, proceeded to delve into exploring the possibilities of "highly sensitive." In their first major study, published in 1997, in the Journal of Personality and Social Psychology, a top peer reviewed journal, they detailed a series of seven studies that they conducted using diverse measures and samples.[1] The study found that there was substantial evidence for a unidimensional core variable that they termed Sensory Processing Sensitivity (SPS), as a descriptive moniker.

Sensory Processing Sensitivity was determined to be partially independent of social introversion and emotionality. This delineation was important because, prior to this study, other personality researchers had thought it to be part of introversion or emotionality or had confused its actual nature in previous studies. Two distinct groups of highly sensitive people emerged: one that seemed to have experienced an unhappy childhood, and a second larger group, who seemed to be similar to those without the trait, except for their high sensitivity. Being a male also seemed to moderate the trait, an important point for us in this book.

The study introduced and validated a 27 item Highly Sensitive Person Scale, which is used to help determine if people may identify with being highly sensitive. The HSP Scale has since been questioned extensively, but still seems to show that the scale is a valid measure that we may use to determine if we may be highly sensitive. As with many aspects of scientific inquiry, researchers are still looking at ways to improve the categories and items that the HSP Scale measures, to ensure that it remains valid, even as we continue to learn new variations and viewpoints on high sensitivity.

Sensory Processing Sensitivity is a neutral genetic trait, or temperament, that is:

- present in over 100 species

- equally divided between males and females

- presents with about 70% introverted and 30% extraverted

- presents with about 50% as high in another genetic trait: sensation seeking

- is deeply affected by early childhood experiences, especially Adverse Childhood Experiences (ACEs), but also positive, supportive early environments

- is fueled by strong, quick emotions, leading to more elaborate processing of stimulation and experiences, in the brain

- reflects a dual strategy for addressing stimuli: reactive, sensitive, responsive, and reflective versus nonresponsive, less reactive, less sensitive, and impulsive.

One strategy is not necessarily better than another, just different. The variety of survival strategies are evolutionary adaptations that enabled our ancestral hunter-gatherer ancestors to exhibit a wider reaction norm, as a group, to survival threats and opportunities. For example, unknown sounds tend to cause some people to advance and check out the source of the noise, while others would prefer to observe and gather more information before acting.

Both strategies are necessary to counterbalance impulsivity and the longer process of observing, reflecting, and weighing options before proceeding. In that regard, if a person is too impulsive, he ran the risk of facing the truly unknown (a dangerous predator, for example); too much reflection and the opportunity may have been missed for a meal (an easy catch, for example), or the threat became realized too late, with drastic consequences!

Animal research has shown that fruit flies, for example, seem to have two strategies: sitters and rovers.

Pumpkinseed sunfish may be bold or timid, and primates may be laid back or uptight.[1] The important point here is that the advantage is only gained through the reflective group being in the minority. If the advantage were too great, it would no longer represent an asset because everyone would know the shortcut or where the best fruits ripen and when. Nature always varies a theme, rather than reinventing the wheel each time. The Emu, the Rhea, and the venerable Ostrich are all the same bird, but separated on different continents after the breakup of the supercontinent, Pangea. Environmental conditions dictated unique factors for each variation of what we think of as the Ostrich.

Similarly, for humans, we developed adaptations that enhanced our survivability and reproductive success in ancestral times when there was an advantage to be had by such a trait. SPS may be thought of as an evolutionary advantage for parents who have some children who are more responsive and some who are less responsive. By dispersing several adaptations throughout a family, nature employs different survival strategies to enable the potential viability of a species.

SPS may best be considered as the D.O.E.S. acronym:

Depth of processing of all stimuli: Highly sensitive people process stimulation in a more elaborate way in the mind and spend more time considering options before acting.

Overstimulation: Along with a greater sensitivity to stimuli comes a tendency for overstimulation. Not all HSPs are alike; some dislike certain smells, bright lights, or scratchy fabrics, while others have no issue with the same stimuli. Overstimulation is highly variable among HSPs. Think of overstimulation as a lower threshold for feeling frazzled or irritated.

Emotional responsiveness and high empathy: HSPs have a wider reaction norm of possible responses, meaning that they may experience several emotions at once quite intensely, rather than a single emotion. This can, obviously, lead to overstimulation when coping skills are not present or effective. HSPs are seemingly hardwired for greater empathy. Empathy is the capacity to enter the emotional and affective states of other people, while experiencing a measurable degree of similitude. This may, as well, lead to overstimulation and HSPs must be careful to manage the levels of energy they take in from others. They must also take care to clear negative energies, so as not to simply become a storage battery of other people's energies, negative and positive. Self-care is essential.

Sensitivity to subtleties: HSPs spend more time noticing visual and other sensory details, often scanning a visual scene for nuance and patterns that others may miss or overlook altogether. This sensitivity may be quite exquisite and HSPs may be quite good at distinguishing between smells, sounds, or visual cues, though they do not possess extra special senses in any way. It's simply the way the same stimulation that we all receive is processed that counts as an advantage for the HSP, on average.

Vantage Sensitivity and Differential Susceptibility

Further evolutions of SPS, by researchers Pluess and Belsky, have seemed to provide credibility for the role that positive and negative environments play for HSPs. It's long been assumed that HSPs did less well in negative environments, as they would quickly feel overwhelmed, overstimulated, and spend more time thinking and feeling the negativity than in those without the trait. However, Pluess and Belsky have pushed it further and confirmed that, in fact, HSPs do much better in positive environments than in those without the trait. They began with Differential Susceptibility as an initial construct to determine how children with sensitivity markers fared in both positive and negative out-of-home care environments. [2] Pluess and Belsky found, quite surprisingly, that contrary to popular belief, sensitive children fared better than those without the trait, leading them to a general notion that sensitive children are especially at-risk in negative environments of all kinds. In other words, they were susceptible to strong influences from both positive and negative environments, or more responsive to *everything.*

Numerous subsequent studies have confirmed this finding, leading the researchers to coin a new term for the construct: Vantage Sensitivity.[3] The term, vantage, in this instance, was chosen to imply a general advantage beyond any singular advantage one might have, such as high intelligence, social standing, or circumstantial upper hand.

Vantage Sensitivity has become something of a breakthrough since the studies have involved thousands of subjects and dozens of studies replicating the findings. It does seem that HSPs in positive environments, especially HS children, will fare as well or better than their counterparts without the trait. This is of tremendous importance to society as we have the opportunity to shape environments for children, and adults, that allow them to flourish and blossom.

Brain Studies

Technology has also provided tools that have enabled scientists to peer inside the brains of HSPs, while hooked up to devices called functional magnetic resonance imaging machines (fMRIs). With fMRI's, researchers have been able to observe areas of the brain that light up when exposed to specific stimuli, like images of loved ones. Areas that light up tend to be involved with mirror neurons, awareness, self-other processing, secondary visual processing, fine visual distinctions, meaning making, and inputs to the autonomic nervous system affecting emotional response.[4]

fMRI studies also seem to demonstrate that SPS moderates the function of culture, as subjects were asked to perform a task that required ignoring cultural context, to accurately answer the questions being posed. Results seem to indicate that SPS, again, serves to filter brain response to sensory information, regardless of cultural context, more so than for subjects of low sensitivity.[5]

What this implies is that HSPs seem to ignore the cultural programming we are all exposed to and, instead, prefer to work out original solutions. The studies also seem to point out the way the brains of HSPs work in a slightly different way. This different viewpoint of brain function in humans opens us up to the possibility that our species needs a minority who process events and stimulation in a slightly different way that allows for more thorough processing, reflection, connecting with others, and pausing to think before acting. Rather than employing a single survival strategy for a species, nature seems to vary in theme so if one approach does not work well enough, there is always a minority whose approach may be better suited to the task at hand. SPS is likely a complementary survival strategy that co-exists along with other strategies.

Survival Strategies, Traits, and Adaptations

Hand in hand with our discussion of brain research is a brief explanation of survival strategies and natural selection. Natural selection is the process by which traits that enable survival of a species are preserved in the genome and passed down from generation to generation. If a trait, on average, facilitates either an advantage in survival or reproduction, it likely gets passed down to enable future generations to benefit. To dig into this further, natural selection produced two broad classes of evolved variants: those playing a role in *survival* and those related to *reproductive* competition. Those variants that interfered with successful adaptation were filtered out, while those that were tributary to the successful solution to an adaptive problem passed through the selection sieve and remained. The filtering process of many generations, interacting with the social, physical, and internal environment, produced characteristics that promoted the reproduction of those who possessed the variants. These may be termed as *adaptations*.[6]

Adaptations are evolved psychological mechanisms that consist of processes addressing a specific survival or reproduction problem in our ancestral past. Adaptations work out of conscious awareness and may only address a specific problem. This specificity differs from generality in that greater focus on one type of problem yields issue-specific solutions that yield an advantage on average. Note that phrase "on average" because an adaptation does not need to have been an advantage in all situations, just on average. Specific solutions require less energy and time to arrive at a solution, thus, are a more efficient expenditure. Sensory processing sensitivity is a trait that generally requires greater time and energy to process stimulation. However, the advantage may be that it will arrive at better long-term solutions that consider many of the aspects in the core of the trait: the four D.O.E.S. aspects.

SPS also likely provided an advantage in facilitating a wider possible range of human behaviors that increased our ability to perform well in context-specific ways. The greater the repertoire, the more options one has available at any given time. SPS remained in the genome because there is still a need for it in human civilization, though we must acknowledge how vastly we humans have altered our lives and the context within which we live them. Moving from an "out of doors" life to one where the elements no longer affected human civilization quite as much, dramatically altered the way we interact, how we view ourselves, and how we live our lives.

With our discussion of brain research, survival strategies, adaptations, and traits complete we are naturally led to consider the role of heritability for SPS. Do we inherit SPS from our parents?   What genes are responsible for SPS?

Genetic Correlates

Sensory processing sensitivity is likely heritable. One recent article that used a classic twin design methodology with 2,686 adolescent twins found that sensitivity has a heritability of .47, which is significant for a trait. [7] Researchers at the University of Copenhagen propose that

SPS "may describe an underlying characteristic more directly associated with the 5-HTTLPR genotype. SPS is associated with the enhanced neural processing of detailed visual stimuli and increased neural activation in response to happy and sad faces. This research has also proposed that several of the defining characteristics of SPS are similar to physiological characteristics found in 5-HTTLPR short allele carriers, including increased brain activation in response to emotional stimuli, increased startle response, and increased cortical response to social evaluation. These researchers believe that high levels of SPS may reflect an endophenotype associated with the serotonin transporter, 5-HTTLPR short/short genotype."[8]

The conclusion of the Copenhagen study indicates that SPS "describes a psychological profile associated with the homozygotic status of a common polymorphism in the serotonin system."[9] Another study, conducted at Beijing Normal University, found that polymorphisms in TH, DBH, SLC6A3, DRD2, NLN, NTSR1, and NTSR2 were associated with SPS. As with many traits, it is likely there is more than one gene influencing how the various aspects of each trait are expressed. SPS is a complex construct that confounds many people, even HSPs, due to the complexity of description of the trait.

We should also acknowledge that the way a trait expresses in a given generation is determined by a number of factors such as the external environment, the early social environment, and, later, personal choices that each person makes throughout the life course. Genetics is one factor to consider but HS men are not their genes and are not their environment.

Key challenge issues for HSPs:

Easily over aroused

HSPs may be easily over aroused by any of a number of stimuli that are unique in each case. This tendency toward over arousal is a significant problem area for most HSPs as they attempt to navigate a world that is increasingly noisy and inconsiderate of personal space, privacy, and even the need to distinguish between formal and informal. HSPs, as a result, often find themselves reacting to unwanted stimuli. This reaction may be annoyance, irritation, fright, and even anger.

Over arousal in social situations for both introverted and extraverted HSPs may be a significant issue that requires careful management. HSPs typically learn to pick and choose the events they attend, knowing that they will likely face over arousal at some point, or for the entire event, such as a concert, and need to recharge later in a quiet space. This need for quiet and isolation may be misread by others who may be less sensitive.

Stronger emotional reactions

Sensory processing sensitivity seems to work by a physical stimulus that sets off the cascade of deep processing in the brain. Strong quick emotions mark the trait and, hand-in-hand with over arousal, the strong feelings may quickly lead to over arousal and an HSP may need to withdraw as a self-protective measure.

HSPs may also feel quite strongly when encountering injustice and may react quite intensely, though this may take various forms in different people. HSPs may also experience stronger emotional reactions as compared to less sensitive people, which may make them feel as if they are different or broken in some way. This faulty perception may be fed by early experiences with stigmatization and lead to low self-esteem and low self-confidence.

Low self esteem

Highly sensitive people from supportive childhoods and environments may be as self-efficacious as anyone else, but those from unsupportive or abusive, neglectful, or traumatic childhoods may feel a deep sense of low self-esteem. To maintain a healthy sense of self-esteem, or a feeling of confidence in one's value or worth, most people do better when they regularly encounter challenging tasks that reinforce their ability to overcome obstacles, to innovate and apply solutions to tasks, and to reinforce that working together means we value each person for their contributions.

The issue for many HSPs is confounded by a need to protect oneself from over arousal while indulging one's curiosity and capacities. Low self-esteem will obviously hamper one's willingness to see a challenging task as desirable and may lead to a self-perpetuating cycle of fewer accomplishments leading to fewer opportunities and challenges.

Wrong lifestyle

Many HSPs spend too much time in lifestyles they are pushed into by culture, which seeks to mold and shape people through its communication and imprinting of values, norms, and beliefs. Culture, and the social groups we each inhabit, often apply peer pressures to conform to ways of being that are at odds with how HSPs feel themselves to be. It may take several decades of adult life before many HSPs reach a point of self-awareness and sufficient self-esteem where they understand the lifestyle they need and have the courage and willingness to make the often-dramatic changes needed to build a lifestyle that fits them.

HSPs often require significant help with establishing and enforcing boundaries, which may also lead to wrong lifestyle choices, i.e., getting married to the wrong partner, choosing the wrong career, or belonging to social groups that do not provide adequate supports throughout life.

Overreactions to criticism

Concurrent with wrong lifestyle choices, many HSPs may also overreact to criticisms, especially when those criticisms feel personal. The strong, quick emotions HSPs experience may lead to an outsize reaction to what feels like an attack. Over arousal can be a quick result of criticisms that are not provided as meaningful critiques meant to be timely, actionable, or substantive. When an HSP feels attacked the tendency is either to flee, prepare to fight, or freeze. This primitive reaction is hardwired into us and is meant to enable our survival in threatening situations. However, in modern societies people are often physically closer together for longer periods of time than in our ancestral past when there was more space between people and groups.

Meeting others

Highly sensitive people may be leery of meeting new people and may prefer to observe a person's demeanor for some time before attempting to make any connections. Most HSPs are introverted, meaning that they prefer to process their experiences internally rather than externally. This intense inner focus may feel quite valued by the individual and he may be reticent to allow others in, both as a means of avoiding over arousal and because he may prefer truly meaningful connections and conversations over superficial ones.

Extraverted HSPs may be just as sociable as any other extravert but may feel a need to withdraw before others to recharge in quiet. Extraverted HSPs may find it easier to meet people but may be just as selective in who they allow into their lives because the underlying sensitive trait still heavily influences their daily energy budget.

Fear of commitment

Meeting others may be a real challenge for HSPs, but even after a friendship has been established, there may be a real fear of commitment, especially for people who have been disappointed or hurt in previous relationships. The experience of betrayal, hurt, or loss may deeply affect how an HSP may feel about future relationships of all kinds.

HSPs also tend to be more aware of the complexities of relationships than less sensitive people and may feel a sense of doubt regarding the viability of long-term relationships. The fear of commitment may be a strong indication that allowing oneself to be open and vulnerable to another person is a more dramatic risk than what might be warranted. This does not mean that HSPs fear relationships in general; indeed, they may be some of the most loyal of friends or partners once they do choose to commit.

Shyness

Feeling apprehensive, awkward, or hesitant around other people may feel quite natural for many HSPs as the trait is about observing before acting or pausing to check. Shyness may be normal for many HSPs, and many do tend to become less hesitant, awkward, or apprehensive over time and with life experience but others may retain shyness throughout life. This may lead to the perpetuation of many issues for HSPs such as low self-esteem, lack of confidence, lack of opportunity and career advancement, and fewer opportunities to meet others.

Working with conflict

Highly sensitive people are, by nature, more empathetic than less sensitive people but may also be less skilled in conflict management due to less experience or because they feel overwhelmed by the emotions of conflict and prefer to avoid it at all costs. Learning to work through and with conflicts can be a key challenge area for HSPs, but also a key strength area as they learn to use their high empathy to understand the other person's point of view.

<u>Key opportunity areas for HSPs:</u>

Creative thinking

Highly sensitive people, by definition of the trait, are likely very good creative thinkers. Noticing subtleties that others miss, thinking about things deeply, having a broader possible range of emotional responses, and greater openness to new ideas defines creativity in general.

Creative thinking is thinking that is expansive, open, and inclusive, but also presumes that one has the rational thinking capacities to evaluate and rank the options, alternatives, and possibilities generated. HSPs, like anyone else, may need to work to improve their critical thinking skills as a necessary complement to creative thinking, but the two combined are a powerful combination!

Empathy/compassion

The ability to relate to the experiences of another person, to enter another person's emotional states as if they were one's own, may be a unique attribute of HSPs but whether that empathy leads to compassionate action is another matter. Empathy should lead to compassion ideally but the need to avoid over arousal is always on the minds of HSPs and may lead them to feel empathy but not act on it. This may be a self-protective measure to avoid depleting their daily energy budgets or simply because feeling another person's experience does not necessarily necessitate an action.

Empathy, in a broader sense, is a key strength for HSPs and is one that is a hallmark of the trait yet is equally part strength and part challenge. Empathy may help make HSPs exceptional at relating to others in ways that feel authentic and real.

Better planners

Highly sensitive people need, as one of their top priorities, for everything they work on to be done well. HSPs may be perfectionists in their work as they note details that others tend to overlook, or they describe the implications and consequences of a particular action. HSPs naturally embody conscientiousness and will not be happy in sloppy environments or following poor plans, or poor leaders.   HSPs make terrific leaders, scientists, managers, teachers, and coordinators, to mention a few, as their eye for both detail and the big picture allows them to see both the forest and the trees.

Healers for the overall community

Highly sensitive people are in a privileged position to a degree by their ability to perceive subtleties that others miss.   These interpersonal, environmental, or subtle energetic cues may provide key information about the state of a given relationship or individual before others catch on, making HSPs ideal as healers of all kinds.

Highly sensitive people may have a keen sense of what people need to hear before they even know it and that may provide HSPs with valuable influence that can be used to harmonize group dynamics, head off issues before they become conflagrations, and negotiate peace between disparate individuals. It is no surprise that many HSPs tend to choose what may be thought of as the helping professions as their career.   Careers like medicine, education, healthcare, and counseling all have an immediate and tangible impact on the lives of others.

Intersection of Sensation Seeking

There is another trait that is important to elucidate early on in our discussion; namely, sensation seeking. Up to 50% of HSPs are also high in sensation seeking which is a separate trait that contrasts quite markedly with sensitivity.

Four aspects of SS

- Thrill and adventure seeking
- Novelty and new experience seeking
- Boredom susceptibility
- Disinhibition[10]

Similar to SPS, people often latch onto the most recognizable feature and fail to appreciate that sensation seeking has four aspects. The one most easily seized upon by many people is thrill and adventure seeking, yet many people identify more closely with novelty seeking, boredom susceptibility, and disinhibition than seeking physical thrills. HSPs, for example, are rarely thrill and adventure seekers, at least not at extreme levels like sky diving, bungee jumping, or drag racing, but will identify with novelty seeking and boredom susceptibility.

High sensation seeking highly sensitive people share influences from two competing traits with the result that sensation seeking often wins out, at the expense of the sensitive.

How males experience SPS and SS

HS men in Western cultures find that sensation seeking is generally more approved of as a desirable trait than sensitivity. Males are further encouraged to extend their natural inclinations toward risk-taking to a higher level with sensation seeking.[11] There are clear issues that arise when a trait like sensation seeking is expressed in an extreme form. Most significant is that risk taking, taken to an extreme, means caution has often been set aside, which entails personal, legal, and financial risks to the individual. Sensation seeking is also a fairly strong trait in driving behavioral choices and, while related to impulsivity, is not the same. Behavioral choices that have a high cost always exact a toll on the well-being of any individual. Sensitive sensation seekers are no exception.

Being highly sensitive expresses itself as a pause to check impulse before acting on stimuli; sensation seeking is more of a "let's check it out" feeling motivated by the dopamine rush one may receive if the stimulation is thrilling in some way. Sensation seeking works through the pleasure pathway in the brain, causing humans to experience a feeling of elation or excitement when it is indulged. For example, many sensation seekers who are high in novelty and new experience seeking will often travel to out of the way places for the unique quality of the experience. They will often seek out the unusual and novel stimulation that comes with encountering new people, places, and events that promise that rush of excitement.

The sensitive sensation seeking man often finds that sensation seeking is higher in younger ages and tends to decline somewhat with age, with only boredom susceptibility remaining for life.[11] Sensitivity, on the other hand, tends to increase as we age, perhaps as a result of an accumulated lack of patience with overstimulation, or an increased focus on the inner lives of older sensitive sensation seekers. Regardless of how we choose to view it, sensation seeking is a contrasting trait with sensitivity, and one must work to understand and appreciate the potential inherent in both traits, without allowing one to utterly dominate the other.

For sensitive sensation seeking men, the challenge is finding ways to hold both traits in suspension equally. Embodying both traits imbues significant capacities that may be developed in time. Among them are a driven sense of creativity, motivated by a restless need to reinvent oneself, thorough processing of experiences and events, and a give and take between risk-taking - which can be quite healthy - and mitigating risk so that it feels safer. To say that being a sensitive sensation seeker is like being two people at once is not an understatement because many such people do feel simultaneously pushed and pulled in competing directions at once. The trick lies in bringing both traits to conscious awareness and making choices that allows for equal development of both traits.

Conclusion

In this first chapter, we have introduced sensory processing sensitivity and said that it is a neutral genetic trait shared by about 15-20% of the world's population. We have reviewed brain research, genetic correlates, and discussed challenge and opportunity areas for sensory processing sensitivity. We have also looked at a separate trait that about 30% of HSPs share: sensation seeking. With this grounding of SPS in the best science we have at the moment, we can proceed on to examine the history and nature of masculinity in our next chapter and expand our discussion of HS men from there.

It is important to note that scientific research is ever-changing and evolving. New studies are being conducted as we speak, and new understandings are expanding our understanding of SPS. With this in mind, we should feel confident in the fact that all the studies to date have helped validate SPS in its original conceptualization. SPS may evolve over time, but the basic core of the trait seems to be very stable and well-researched. As with all research, we should keep an open mind and use the knowledge that has been so hard won to improve our lives and the lives of our families, communities and the world.

Questions and answers

Is Sensory Processing Sensitivity a disorder?

No, SPS is not a disorder at all, it's simply a neutral genetic trait. SPS does not appear in the DSM, the manual that psychotherapists refer to for diagnosing disorders, and does not require treatment of any kind. Being highly self-aware of what it means to be highly sensitive will help you to navigate life better and help you to realize your potential throughout your life's course. SPS is not to be confused with Sensory Processing Disorder, which does appear in the DSM.

How many men are highly sensitive?

Sensory processing sensitivity is evenly dispersed among males and females, with men comprising half of the 15-20% of the highly sensitive population worldwide.

Are highly sensitive men gay?

Some are but the percentage is presumed to be similar to the overall population. HS men may be straight, gay, bisexual, or any other preference, just as in the rest of the population. As a neutral trait, SPS does not predispose one toward any sexual preference or identity. For those HS men who are gay, they face the additional challenge of how to embrace their identities as both gay men and HS men.

What are the best books on highly sensitive people and sensation seekers?

There are a number of good books and now, two documentary movies on sensory processing sensitivity. The movies are called *Sensitive-The Untold Story* and *Sensitive and in Love*. *Sensitive-The Untold Story* is available to rent/buy at https://sensitive-theuntoldstory.vhx.tv/buy/sensitive-the-untold-story-1 and *Sensitive and in Love* is available to rent/buy at https://sensitiveandinlove.com/.

A good list of books for <u>sensory processing sensitivity</u> includes:

Elaine Aron – The Highly Sensitive Person.

The Highly Sensitive Parent

The Highly Sensitive Person in Love.

The Highly Sensitive Person's Workbook.

The Highly Sensitive Child: Helping Our Children Thrive When the World Overwhelms Them.

The Highly Sensitive Person's Survival Guide: Essential Skills for Living Well in an Overstimulating World (co-written with Ted Zeff).

Psychotherapy and the highly sensitive person: Improving outcomes for that minority of people who are the majority of clients.

Ted Zeff – The Strong Sensitive Boy.

The Power of Sensitivity.

Raise an Emotionally Healthy Boy.

Tom Falkenstein – The Highly Sensitive Man

Tracy Cooper – Thrive: The Highly Sensitive Person and Career.

Thrill: The High Sensation Seeking Highly Sensitive Person

Barrie Jaeger – Making Work Work for the Highly Sensitive Person.

A good list of <u>peer-reviewed research papers</u> (for those interested in the hardcore science behind SPS):

Elaine Aron – Sensory processing sensitivity and its relation to introversion and emotionality (Journal of Personality and Social Psychology, issue 73).

Sensory processing sensitivity: A review in the light of the evolution of biological responsivity (Personality and Social Psychology Review, Issue 16).

The clinical implications of Jung's concept of sensitiveness (Journal of Jungian Theory and Practice, Issue 8).

The highly sensitive brain: An fMRI study of sensory processing sensitivity and response to others' emotions (Brain and Behavior, Issue 4).

Revisiting Jung's concept of innate sensitiveness (Journal of Analytical Psychology, Issue 49).

Jay Belsky and **Michael Pluess**

Beyond diathesis stress: differential susceptibility to environmental influences (Psychological Bulletin, Issue 135).

Vantage sensitivity: individual differences in response to positive experiences (Psychological Bulletin, Issue 139).

For **<u>sensation seeking</u>** the list includes:

<u>Books</u>

Marvin Zuckerman

Behavioral expressions and biosocial bases of sensation seeking.

Sensation seeking and risky behavior.

<u>Peer-reviewed research papers</u>

Marvin Zuckerman

Dimensions of sensation seeking (Journal of consulting and clinical psychology, Issue 36).

Jonathan Roberti

A review of behavioral and biological correlates of sensation seeking (Journal of Research in Personality, Issue 38).

Agnes Norbury and **Masud Husain**

Sensation seeking: dopaminergic modulation and risk for psychopathology (Behavioral Brain Research, Issue 288).

Marcus Munafo, Binnaz Yalcin, Saffron Willis-Owen, and **Jonathan Flint**

Association of the D4 receptor gene (DRD4) and approach-related personality traits: A meta-analysis and new data.

Rick Hoyle, Michael Stephenson, Philip Palmgreen, Elizabeth Lorch, and **R. Donohew**

Reliability and validity of a brief measure of sensation seeking (Personality and Individual Differences, Issue 32).

Chunhui Chen, et al

Contributions of dopamine-related genes and environmental factors to highly sensitive personality: a multi-step neuronal system-level approach (PlosOne, Issue 6).

There are many others, but this list serves as a great start towards a better understanding of sensory processing sensitivity and related topics (gender, career, alternative conceptualizations).

<u>Empowerment Points</u>

- Sensory processing sensitivity is a naturally occurring genetic trait, or temperament, that is present in at least 100 other species.
- The four core aspects of SPS are thorough processing of all stimulation, overstimulation in certain individualized circumstances, high empathy and emotional responsiveness, and sensitivity to subtleties. One needs all four to truly be highly sensitive.
- Seventy percent of HSPs are introverted, 30% are extraverted, and about 30% are high in sensation seeking as well as SPS.
- SPS is divided equally between males and females.

- SPS is a survival strategy that likely evolved in our ancestral past to enable the survival and reproduction of the species.
- Sensation seeking is a separate trait about 30% of HSPs share along with SPS.
- Sensation seeking has four key aspects: thrill and adventure seeking, novelty and new experience seeking, boredom susceptibility, and disinhibition. One does not need to be high in all four to be considered high in sensation seeking.

CHAPTER 2

A Very Brief History of Masculinity

"But by far the worst thing we do to males — by making them feel they have to be hard — is that we leave them with very fragile egos. The harder a man feels compelled to be, the weaker his ego is." — Chimamanda Ngozi Adichie

Before we begin to unravel the complex construct that is known to us as masculinity, we should first, very carefully, define what we mean by the term "masculinity." Masculinity, like all social concepts, has a unique history that we must acknowledge and appreciate in order to contextualize how we interpret it today. It's been said that "masculinity means different things to different people in different places at different times,"[12] leaving us with the difficult task of deciding which people we are referring to, where they live, and what time period their thinking evolved in. Here, my intention is to refer primarily to masculinity in the United States and to people from the 20th and 21st centuries. Masculinity in this sense is not a singular term: we should more appropriately say "masculinities" to be more accurate, but for simplicity's sake we will use "masculinity" acknowledging that we are limited by language.

Masculinity, likewise, seems to refer to an adjective, as if masculinity were a thing, rather than a process. The English language is obsessed with tacking adjectives onto every possible entity, regardless of appropriateness. Masculinity, in practical reality, is a process people engage in acting out through their embodiment of certain attributes or traits that demonstrate identification with this overall construct.[13] Rather than take masculinity as a given, with no further explanation needed, let's play devil's advocate and assume that masculinity is a process that varies by people, place, and time. In doing so, we open up the rich possibilities in open-ended exploration.

Here, we do not presume to know the answers to the problems we face in weighing masculinity against the demands of the current world. Rather, we assume a "not-knowing" stance, whereby we will consider new possibilities that may be generative of new perspectives and different views. Readers will have to consider the concepts presented, weigh their relative logic (considering how well-reasoned they are) and decide for themselves how masculinity has been embodied in their time, place, and among their people.

Since culture is ever evolving, we are all active participants in deciding what culture will look like in the future. That provides each of us with an equal opportunity in choosing to subscribe to a set of beliefs regarding masculinity, to choose new beliefs, or to build a new middle ground where some beliefs are maintained while others are disavowed. In the end, we do have much to say regarding our expectations of masculinity and how we choose to embody it and support it in others.

A Very Brief History of Masculinity

Hunter-Gatherers

Through the timeline of human history various conceptualizations of masculinity have always existed. For the hunter-gatherers, the earliest known subsistence method, life may have been more egalitarian with joint efforts between men and women to secure a tribe's (or group's) daily nutritional needs.[14] With no emphasis on any one person possessing or acquiring a surplus (this is tough to do in an age with little to no preservation technology) the goal was mutual cooperation for survival's sake. There are very interesting instances where survival required less daily energetic expenditures, namely, native tribes along the Northwest Coast of North America. In these tribes, since the luxury of time allowed for the development of culture (and some very sophisticated art forms), people chose a social structure that differed from those who spent more time in subsistence hunting/gathering. You might be surprised to know that some groups chose a matrilineal society (female leaders).

Among the Haida, an indigenous people of the Northwest Coast scattered among the many islands of Haida Gwaii (or islands of the people), life is nurtured by the ocean and heavy coniferous forests with less time required to obtain resources. In such a condition, the Haida people lived for nearly 17,000 years, albeit with tremendous disruption during thc Colonial Period when their way of life was under attack. Choosing a matrilineal societal structure, in this case, provides for lineage transfer on the mother's side, often through distant relations.[15] The Haida were not an inactive group. Instead, they constructed ocean-going war canoes, some large enough to accommodate 60 rowers and swift enough to engage enemies with sophisticated weapons fit for canoe warfare. Haida society differed from more intensive hunter/gatherer groups in that they developed stratification between groups, even between individuals.

Stratification is precisely what separates and isolates groups of people, who then go on to develop vastly different ways of thinking and viewing the world. Stratification also leads to inequality as people begin to acquire wealth, status, and power over others.[16] Hunter-gatherers may have embodied the most egalitarian and balanced system possible for human beings that allowed each person to contribute to the tribe's needs in ways that acknowledged relative skills and temperaments. For example, some hunters are very proficient at reading the signs of animal tracks and being able to discern crucial information like age of the track, direction, type of animal, even health of the animal, which all contributed to a successful hunt.

Similarly, risk-takers may have inherently preferred to be "on the move" and serve as hunters rather than stay in the camp and engage in less risky activities. There is a downside, of course, to the hunting strategy: often, hunters returned home with no success, or little success. Gatherers, on the other hand, usually enjoyed some success at foraging for foodstuffs, depending on the time of year and the exact area. Moving with animal herds, such as the Plains Indians in North America, meant a steady food supply, but a strategy based on hunting a given area then moving to the next was likely unpredictable at best.

There were two different approaches to return on labor among hunter-gatherer groups: delayed return and immediate return. Delayed return emphasized more of a division of labor based on technology and potential inequalities as men assumed authority positions, often through aggression, and immediate return emphasizing movement and relative equality, since there was no central authority necessary. The more complex societies became, the greater the inequalities between the sexes began to emerge as men accumulated wealth, prestige, and power over others.[17]

Separate spheres between the sexes, based on the division of labor, helped form the basis for gender as a role that was to be played out.[18] The hunter-gatherer strategy was our predominant survival strategy for a far longer time than what would come next: the agriculturists.

Agriculturalists and Civilizations

Over time, people realized the advantages of staying in one area and cultivating that land to grow plants. They also learned that domesticating animals and animal husbandry was a far more predictable way to live than being subject to climate changes, droughts, floods, etc. Once we learned to farm and ranch, we became agriculturalists and we were tied to specific places. This new paradigm enabled the advantages of accumulated knowledge that could be passed down in writing and the development of culture. Living in one area also brought about greater stratification and inequality as people became rapidly unequal in terms of power, prestige, and place. The shift from more egalitarian, where male and female roles were more equal, to one where they became less equal, established new demands on masculinity.

Greater population densities changed our fundamental relationship with the land and the resources it could provide, with men taking on roles that involved power, while women were burdened with the demand for more hands to tend to the additional workload in the form of children. This unequal division of power sharing roles seems to have led to the idea that men were the natural leaders due to their sheer numbers in positions of power.[17]

Patriarchal systems began to emerge over time and laid the foundations for greater sophistication that transformed agrarian societies into civilizations with trade, leaders, and, eventually, bureaucracies. With civilizations came the formal declarations of men as dominant over women and individual cultures pitted against other cultures, often engaging in warfare and conflict.[19] The surplus that resulted from better cultivation and preservation methods brought on greater inequalities between male and female and between what would become social classes.

Men, in this period, cemented the notions that male and female were naturally unequal, and did so by controlling what one heard, said, or did. When the balance of power is in the hands of those with an agenda, propaganda is often the preferred means used to perpetuate the illusion of natural rights. The imbalance of power continues to this day and plays out before our eyes as women and unequal groups struggle for greater equality, while the power elites work to ensure their status as the dominant group in society.[20]

The Turning Point – The Industrial Revolution

The movement from an agrarian society to one with a surplus where power, position, and prestige became dominant factors in who controlled the levers of power, including who decided the formulation of gender roles, accelerated with the rapid development of technology that led us to a swift change from rural to a society that was more urban, more dependent, and more unequal and divided.

Culture, as it developed between 1750-1914 CE, owed much to separate nation states that developed quite different ideals about gender, sex, and social roles. Increasing literacy brought the idea of rationality to the forefront as Kant differentiated reason as separate from nature, with what is human thought of as rational and what is nature disdained as animal. Since women were thought to be closer to nature through childbearing, men were presumed to be more rational and, thus, to lead in the battle to subjugate the natural world.

Reason and emotion were similarly differentiated, with men exhibiting less emotion, feeling, and wants, which were associated with an animal body, and religion decried emotion as inferior and unnatural.[21] Women, in this sense, were less in control of emotion, feeling, and wants and, thus, kept in a subservient role to perpetuate inequalities and a natural order that was anything but natural. By the 19th century, there were two distinct views of manhood: the gentlemanly patriarchy and the rugged artisan.

The gentleman derived his power from holding lands from which he employed others to generate a profit, while the rugged artisan relied on his physical strength and acquired skills to provide compensation and resources.[13] A Puritanical view of masculinity also shifted how men and women interacted and viewed each's respective gender role.

As urbanization began to take hold and people moved into city centers, manhood began to be less about autonomy and self-control to becoming dependent on wages, which entailed less autonomy and less control. For many men, this set up an internal conflict that largely continues to this day where to be dependent is to be "less of a man."[22] In this new capitalist paradigm, men had to constantly "prove their manhood" by fighting with other males for position, power, and influence. Higher earnings and prestige became the new "proof" that one was, indeed, a man.[23]

Masculinity's Lag

Masculinity has largely remained stuck in this industrial age notion of manhood as one that is forever insecure, relentless in its demands for tangible proof of manhood, and, now, behind the curve regarding our post-industrial age.[23] Early 20th century notions of manhood, and separation between the sexes, were heightened by World War 2, when vast numbers of women entered the workforce to "man" the factories and churn out war equipment. Feeling a sense of empowerment, many women expected to continue this newfound sense of independence and autonomy from household confines and narrow expectations, only to be categorically informed in the post-war period that they were no longer needed and should return to their homes and familiar expectations of women. The resulting sense of dissent sparked the women's movement, that directly began to challenge male power in the 1960s.

Men, during the 20th century, especially after the 1960s counterculture movement, felt the seismic shift in women demanding to enter the workforce and find greater equality. This threat to men's traditional source of economic power, always a linchpin in dependence, helped to contribute to a questioning of masculinity and its role in society.[24] As culture has failed to keep up with the pace of technological change, many men find themselves ill-equipped to equally share the stage with women, people of color, and other groups who now fully co-exist in the workplace, and, increasingly, in society in general.

Very simply, when men only had to contend with a limited pool of other men, proving one's manhood was an easier task, but when the game changed and men found themselves less valued and with fewer opportunities the result was a sense of powerlessness and lack of meaning.[25] As other groups in society have advanced, many men find themselves treading water or otherwise unable to take advantage of an information economy where cooperation, mentoring, and nurturing of talent and skills is essential to success.

The workplace is one example of gender role strain, but there are many others that are challenging traditional notions of masculinity; in fact, making it obsolete as the world passes them by. Nostalgia for former times, when things were thought to be easier, simpler, or "fairer" causes many men to resist with political action and violence against those they choose to label as unlike them.

The question becomes, is masculinity necessarily toxic? Or is it how it is enacted by some men? I take the position that masculinity is not toxic, people; however, may make quite poor choices that lead to suffering and inequalities, making it seem as if the gender role is, in and of itself, toxic. We are all active participants in deciding culture through our personal choices, our behaviors, and our actions in the world. People may be toxic, but men, as a distinct segment of the species, are not, simply because we are hard-wired as prosocial beings for cooperation, empathy, and compassion.

Today, we see younger generations of men who seem to be making other choices for how they will embody masculinity and it is encouraging, in many cases, as we see greater cooperation, less anger, and a willingness to eschew past notions of masculinity in favor of more modern realities. The workplace itself has contributed, in large part, to this generational change in attitudes towards masculinity, as men and women, at all levels, have found the utility of embracing aspects of the formerly rigid gender role.

Modern females are often strong, independent, and achievement oriented, while men have found application for mentoring, compassion, and the larger possible mission of corporations as good citizens in the world. Many older generations, meanwhile, may cling to what they know and view the youth through a less than favorable lens. This is, perhaps, an overgeneralization, and, indeed, there are many members of older generations who have always embodied what we now see as a more balanced synergy between gender roles. We should never overlook the many men, from all generations, who have made choices to embody masculinity in healthy and benevolent ways, including my grandfather.

With the shifts in society, women, as well, have had to reflect on what is required of them in the workplace, and in society, as traits normally associated with masculinity, such as aggression, efficiency, goal achievement, and less emotional reflection, become expedient for their lives in a brave new world. Many women today have never known what it meant to be stuck at home in a domesticated life; indeed, today, to subscribe to the notion that a woman's place is in the home, is no longer a mainstream idea.

Women today serve in many traditionally male capacities, ranging from CEO, to policewomen, and combat roles to businesspeople, priests, and leaders in most capacities. This encroachment has had an impact on men's security in their identity as bread winners, protectors, and leaders in society.

Men, in a general sense, tend to work to fulfill the demands of society, but they fail to explore or cultivate their inner selves.[21] This lack of an inner, reflective life where meaning is found through meeting what men perceive as worthy, noble, or justified, is a crisis point for masculinity, and for all of society as males struggle to define a sense of worth within themselves.

There have been a number of men's movements over the past few decades, seeking to redefine, or clarify, what "good men" should represent in society, but none have had any particular staying power as people seem to move quickly from one movement to another. It's as if the clarity seems to dissipate as quickly as it is gained.

The mythopoetic men's movement, as described by Professor Shepherd Bliss, focused on self-help retreats, often in wilderness settings, seeking to reconnect to a lost pre-industrial age of masculinity that was based on the work of psychologist Carl Jung, Robert Bly, Joseph Campbell, and Robert A. Johnson. Professing a gender essentialism strategy that presupposes a natural, deep masculinity, such movements tended to make up for lost societal rituals of entering manhood, and association with appropriate male role models embodying a mature form of masculinity, as opposed to an immature masculinity, that results from males not being afforded opportunities to grow and develop according to their true natures. Largely attended by middle aged white men, who were able to afford such retreats, the movements failed to gain lasting traction because they failed to move beyond engaging men in emotional, therapeutic work.

Questions and answers

Is masculinity toxic?

We hear a lot lately about "toxic masculinity" but, since masculinity is simply a collection of arbitrary beliefs about what constitutes masculinity, whether it is toxic is relative to who is embodying it. Plenty of men are benevolent and as far from toxic as can be. Masculinity can no more be thought of as toxic than femininity can be thought of as toxic. It has been and always will be about the way it is embodied. Humans are prosocial primates and inherently have no self-interest in toxicity. In fact, a benevolent masculinity is to be celebrated and aspired to by men as desirable and attainable. There is nothing inherently toxic about being a male.

Is the idea of HS men the same as New Age men's movements?

Not at all. HS men have been with the human population since the beginning and will be with us as long as the species endures. Sensory Processing Sensitivity simply articulates a distinct genetic trait that had, in the past, been confused with introversion, shyness, or emotionality. Understanding that the HS man is distinctly different simply allows him to be more self-aware and work on translating his potential into positive action.

Empowerment Points

- Masculinity means different things to different people in different times and places

- The shift to agriculture from hunter-gatherer shifted from more egalitarian to stratified and unequal

- Masculinity is largely "stuck" in the industrial age where men had to constantly prove their manhood.

- 21st century masculinity is fully capable of meeting the needs of 21st century people, and beyond.

CHAPTER 3

A Boy's Life – Childhood

"Play is often talked about as if it were a relief from serious learning. But, for children, play is serious learning. Play really is the work of childhood." Fred Rogers

In this chapter, we will seek to explore the ways that early beginnings may affect the lives of highly sensitive boys across the lifespan. It is a well-established fact that negative environments will prove to be detrimental, as we have learned with Adverse Childhood Experiences (ACEs)[26] [27] and Vantage Sensitivity, [28] but a positive early environment may prove to be especially beneficial for the highly sensitive boy.

Within each type of early environment there is a myriad of factors that come into play that we should consider. For example, the family dynamics become very important in how childhood is experienced, including how a highly sensitive boy (HSB) thinks of himself within the family structure and the world.

Throughout this chapter, we will visit quotes derived from a study conducted for this book involving highly sensitive men, who were interviewed at length concerning their lived experiences on a number of fronts. These quotes will help lend the human touch as we see and hear their narratives.

Subtle Awareness of Sensitivity

Childhood, for highly sensitive boys, may be a time of only subtle awareness of their temperament as they play, create, and interact with others. It is only over time that some boys learn that they are different in any meaningful way from other boys. For example, early on, many boys seem to meld into each other in play groups or are otherwise occupied to such an extent that self-reflection is not a prominent feature of their young lives.

Travis: "*I always played with the kids in the neighborhood. I never thought about black or white or anything like that. It was just neighbors and the kids in the neighborhood. I just played ball with the neighbors and didn't even think about it.*"

Tom: "*I think I was too busy learning to notice.*"

Matt: "*I played a lot of ball, rode bikes, and generally did outside stuff with the neighborhood boys and girls. We basically lived outside in the 1970s and were largely on our own.*"

Other boys are aware that they are in some way different but understanding how that fits into a context may take many years.

Tom: "*I am introverted, and my siblings are huge extroverts. I can reckon with these things now as an adult that I couldn't as a child or a teenager. I was introverted and also highly sensitive. Growing up I was the crybaby, that sort of thing. Another piece of the puzzle is that I am a gay person, so it is hard for me to look back and say that I feel different, because that emerged in my teens. It is hard for me to be able to separate out what was sensitivity.*"

Kirk: "*Yes, I did understand that I was different. It was shocking to me, because I basically had the perception that everybody was like me, especially as a boy as I started working through the grades in school. It became more obvious through experience that sensitivity was something that I needed to keep to myself. It was basically a punishable offense, not in school, but with my dad. He was not respectful of that trait in me at all. I began to understand that it was unusual, and I began to understand that it was not acceptable both in terms of how I got along with the other boys and girls to a certain point.*

Matt: *"As a child I recall watching Sunday morning wrestling shows on tv and becoming outraged when the bad guy would cheat. My face would get red, and I would almost cry from the sense of injustice and frustration at clearly seeing cheating. My parents were shocked and would always say that it was "just television" and to calm down. I felt the intensity of the emotion most acutely, even at a young age."*

Christian: *"I never had friends. I mean, I had a hard time keeping friends, and I was always picked on. I always wanted to be a part of a group, but I could never get accepted into a group. I never got invited to parties, that forced me to develop what I have now, basically nothing has ever changed. I just have a rich inner life. I read a lot.*

Books have become my best friend. I feel like I have just been forced to do that. I realized it back in grammar school. Ever since grammar school, I have spent all my time in libraries just reading, instead of playing with the other kids. I realized people were going to pick on me, so I just hid in the library. Libraries were the only safe places for me. I would say that I am a very, very introverted HSP. That is how I learned it. I knew it very early on. It has never come as a surprise once I learned what it was."

Kurt: "A*t the time I felt like I was the only one.*"

Andy: "*It was kind of hard to tell sometimes. I never really made friends very well. I would make better acquaintances and I would have friends for a year or so and then, for whatever reason, go hang out with somebody else. That has been a pattern continuously. Sometimes, I just do things faster than other people and notice things differently or inevitably have a very warped sense of humor.*"

Socialization into Masculinity

It is during our childhoods that we begin to encounter culture through our parents, siblings, and others who reinforce for us what is acceptable behavior and what is not.[29] Of course, culture, as we should note, is an entirely arbitrary construction of human societies and there is no right or wrong way to behave intrinsically.[30] HSBs may learn very early on that their sensitivity is either supported and approved of or not supported and discouraged, even representing punishable behavior as parents attempt to mold and shape their children into what they think they should be to fit a standard of "normal."

There are any number of emotional difficulties that may develop during childhood for HSBs that may last throughout the life course. Several of the most pertinent difficulties for HSBs are a sense of shame, lowered self-esteem, low self-confidence, lack of boundaries, and anxiety.[31] These emotional anchor weights can be quite limiting in the lives of HSBs, and later highly sensitive men, who quite often may still be dealing with unresolved issues around power and status. We might even consider these to be similar to the psychological complexes of Carl Jung and Sigmund Freud, both depth psychologists who described similar issues with one central theme typically serving as the maladaptive influence on our thinking, perceptions, and feelings.[32]

To illustrate this point, let's look at how disapproval from a parent may encourage the conditions for the development of a power complex. Kurt describes how having an alcoholic father led him to develop feelings of lack of stability, due to having to continually be conscious of what might happen next:

Kurt: *"My father was a functioning alcoholic, so he drank a lot. There was a lot of having to do what children of an alcoholic have to do: they have to engage when they come into a room a lot, so I had a lot of anxiety and everyone would go to sleep before me and I would be up all night and would go to school and I couldn't focus. I was just literally in a state, as if everything was a dream. I was basically labeled as kind of a dumb, slow kid. I just wasn't getting enough support in school, but also at home. My parents didn't know what to do because everybody else was excelling. That is the way they (my siblings) escaped from some of the chaos. It was a really damaging stereotype that I was labelled as stupid; I internalized that."*

This complex around believing that he was slow or unintelligent followed Kurt through his school years:

"In high school, I have no idea how I graduated, but I somehow managed to get a C average. I think I barely got by basically. I had one teacher in high school, or a couple, that really took an interest and I actually got B's in their courses, because they took an interest. I was kind of like that kid that was just shut down and even if I knew the

answer, I was afraid to say it. I didn't trust my answer, I didn't want to speak in front of people."

Kurt follows his story of faulty perceptions, lack of self-esteem, and lack of personal power with this statement: "*I think I was that kid that they were trying to connect with, and they couldn't.*" When HSBs experience ACEs and the often negative and unsupportive home environment that goes along with them, they may feel powerless on many fronts and come to believe in faulty notions. They may not believe that they are "smart" and this will be reflected in underachievement. Note, though, how Kurt described doing far better when he had teachers who "took an interest." In positive environments, sensitive boys tend to do significantly better than those without the trait and will, in any event, thrive much better in a positive environment than a negative one.

Kurt continued to slowly push his way forward in life, but never addressed the issues connected to his chaotic childhood until later when he entered therapy and made the realization that he had "internalized this notion that I am a bad person because I am stupid." It was only then that he came to the awareness that he, in fact, was not unintelligent, stupid, or any of the things he had believed about himself stemming from childhood.

Through much internal work, including having to revisit, in a metaphorical sense, his seven-year-old self, Kurt emerged with a clearer sense of self-worth and possibility in life. Kurt was led to practicing psychodrama theater to act out much of the internalized trauma he had carried for so long and in a way that served to help others on their journeys. Even as he progressed, he found that his eagerness and passion for psychodrama pushed him beyond his limits and he reached several burnout points where he realized that he had to learn to set and enforce boundaries for himself.

Support in Childhood – What it Looks like

There are enough Kurt stories that could fill entire books, but we will simply acknowledge the depth to which a chaotic and negative early environment may affect a HSB throughout his life course. Conversely, for HSBs from supportive environments, outcomes may be very different, as with the case of Dale.

"I showed an interest in music early in my life, and my dad was very supportive of that. It is really interesting, because he was really into sports and that kind of thing, but he still supported me. My other siblings played sports and had different pursuits, but my dad, and I read a lot about dad's really pushing into sports or other kind of macho stuff, was not like that. He was extremely supportive of me going into music. He liked music himself. He wasn't a professional musician, but he was supportive, my mother was too."

Dale's parents encouraged and supported their son's interest in music, including providing him with opportunities to take lessons and watch other proficient musicians.

"When I was seven my dad got me a little keyboard. We were church goers and I used to go up and watch the organ player every week. That didn't seem to bother her. She was really sweet about it. When I was seven, or just before I was seven, my dad got me a little thing that is sort of like what we call a keyboard today, and I started playing.

Immediately, I started to play. They provided piano lessons for me by the time I was eight years old."

Dale's early foundation of acceptance and love helped him to thrive later in his school career:

"I was a good student and I enjoyed school. I enjoyed learning, so that part of it was positive. I had a good circle of friends that I shared interests with, and I had good people for friends. It could be that some of those friends were HSP's, that is something to think about. I had a lot of good friends, and I didn't feel lonely or anything like that."

Later, in Dale's college career, he similarly enjoyed friendships that upheld what he experienced early on with his family.

"I had a really good college experience. I went to a small college. It was about six hundred fifty students. The classes were small and most of the time your relationship with your professor was personal. In the music department, it was a pretty close-knit community. I felt well, I did well, and I excelled in the music program. I got along really well with my professors, and I had a good close circle of friends in college that I felt comfortable with. I really loved the learning environment. I love a structured learning environment, so I did really well in college. I just did fine and I had some luck. I had good roommates all four years. I didn't have any struggle with my roommates. I had friends that I had good things in common with. I worked for a church in college, so I had a little bit of income and a good supportive circle of people in the church that I worked for when I was in college."

Years later, Dale learned that he was highly sensitive and that knowledge, for him, was empowering in that it allowed him to have an explanation for why he seemed to experience the world in a slightly different way. Even if a HSB enjoys a supportive childhood, it is important to note that learning about oneself may still take time and effort to explore the literature and resources that are so widely available today.

"I was on Amazon, and I am always trying to come to terms about the emotional stuff that goes on in my life and I came across the Elaine Aaron book. I think it is the one called The Highly Sensitive Person. It kind of fascinated me. I can't remember, I may have gone to her website and done the questionnaire, but I got the book and read it, and it's like, oh my god, this is me! It is like it helped me understand better some of the stuff growing up, some of the dynamics of my life now, some of the things that are going on now. It also helps me to be a little more patient with people who are not HSP."

A supportive early upbringing creates a firm foundation on which to build where the HSB feels comfortable and secure enough in himself and his family to venture out with less anxiety and worry. Knowing that one has a loving and supportive family to return to can make all the difference in how a HSB develops and grows into his capacities over time.[27] Dale is one example but there are many varied examples of HSBs from supportive childhoods who became very successful and happy HSMs.

The "In-Between" Childhood

What if one had some support in childhood, but also experienced some degree of trauma, chaos, or other disorder in the household? This depends on how much it matters to the individual. The key point for highly sensitive men is that we process all experiences in a more elaborate way, feel more deeply, and will likely retain more of the effects of the trauma over the life course. Many HS men, indeed, are able to largely overcome their ACEs and move through life just fine, noting that they are only sensitive with regards to emotional intensity and noting subtleties. The good news, as well, is that HS men may go on to become attentive and loving parents, even if they come from a background of non-approval. In fact, at times, that sort of background can prove to be the catalyst that drives a HS man to do better, to be better, and to not repeat the same mistakes made by parents, or other caregivers.

Culture Hardens Males but SPS Moderates Culture

The research seems to show that boys are uniquely different from girls in important ways. For example, boys tend to take greater risks, engage in more aggressive play, and display a greater physicality than girls. [33] This fundamental difference is later highlighted as boys are influenced by culture. Our early primary group associations, our families, become our first points of reference for modeling acceptable behaviors. It is precisely at this point, where culture begins to intersect with natural traits, that one begins to exert more influence over life than another. In many cases, it tends to be culture that wins.

Highly sensitive boys may find themselves encouraged, cajoled, or expected to engage in risks that they may not feel comfortable with, owing to their trait, which constantly reinforces for them the need to think before acting. This pause to reflect may put him at odds with more impulsive boys who prefer to act first and think later. Always there is a pressure to conform, and sensitive boys are no exception as they are forced to navigate the waters of going along to get along or choosing to walk away and potentially face ridicule for not being "tough enough" or for being "scared."

Highly sensitive boys may react strongly to witnessing violence, conflict, or lack of concern for others.[31] HSBs, because they feel quite intensely and will process that feeling for a longer time, may quickly feel overstimulated or over aroused by what may seem inconsequential to less sensitive boys. The tendency toward over arousal may contribute to making a HSB feel very different than others. Once a HSB begins school and is surrounded by the 80% of the population who are not highly sensitive, it does not take long to begin to note contrasts in behavior.

Sensory processing sensitivity has been postulated to moderate the effects of culture and several studies seem to back this up.[34] It is likely that HSBs, though they are as exposed to the same culture as all boys, do not necessarily feel as compelled to conform to or abide by the dictates of a given culture. This is a generalization, based on research, and it is likely that culture does attempt to, not so subtlety, shape and mold the thoughts, feelings, and behaviors of HSBs. This push-pull dynamic between what HSBs feel they are told they should be and what they feel they ought to be can set up a sense of dissonance that can last throughout childhood and into the teen years.

During the teen years, it's very common for young people to begin questioning their sense of self as they inch closer to young adulthood. Questions that lead to the answer, such as the ones culture provides, only serve to reinforce the notion that HSBs have something "wrong" with them. HSBs are being told that there is only one acceptable framework for being a man and to be less is to not be a man. Ridiculous, of course, but HSBs do hear a lot of "parroting" of the culture from adults, other children, and, especially, the mass media, which is insidious in perpetuating mediocre values.

Highly sensitive boys sometimes do have tolerant, patient, and supportive adult figures in their lives and do learn to embody their sensitive natures in ways that feel confident, but it seems that many HS men report less acceptance of their sensitivity than support. The nature of culture is such that social group pressures can be immense on parents and members of society, and they may feel that they are truly helping a HSB who seems to be different when, in fact, they may be doing more unconscious, though well-intended, harm than good.

The Power of Dads

Fathers have a unique role to play in their HS son's lives. A father's love contributes as much as a mother's love to a child's overall development and is a crucial piece of the puzzle of early childhood acceptance or rejection. In one large scale study, researchers Ronald Rohner and Abdul Khaleque found that children who felt rejected by parents tended to feel "more anxious and insecure, as well as more hostile and aggressive towards others."[35] That childhood pain follows us into adulthood and is similar to physical pain, with the exception that the pain may be relived again and again.

Rohnert and Khaleque found that it is often the father's rejection that is most keenly felt because children may perceive the father to have higher interpersonal power and prestige. If that is the case, it is essential that fathers are aware of their deep influence over their HS son's life and participate in nurturing and childcare to an equal degree as the mother. HSBs will respond especially well to positive nurturing and equal affection from both parents.

My four children are now grown adults, ranging from 20 to 29 years old. I can say that even after one's kids have become adults, they still need our influence, our advice, and our guidance. Our influence is especially needed if our children are also highly sensitive. A dad's wisdom and calming presence can be an anchor for our children as they navigate the challenges of life as a HSB or HSG. Value and treasure your role as a dad because it is one of the most fulfilling and rewarding roles that you will play in this life.

The Power of Mom's

Mothers have a special influence on their sons because boys may wish to please their mothers by living up to what is expected, even if that is at the cost of living an inauthentic life that does not reflect the HSBs true nature. Mothers, in this sense, must be mindful of this power to influence and perpetuate extreme expressions of masculinity. Make no mistake, masculinity in and of itself is as capable of benevolence, positive action, and kindness as femininity, but if certain elements are exaggerated and promoted as being desirable, the result may be misshapen and angry men who possess few of the coping mechanisms that they will need to address the many inevitable obstacles, crises, and challenges life will throw at them.

Females, in general, may also be a factor in perpetuating qualities in men they profess to despise yet blindly promote. The pressure to conform weighs heavily on all members of a society. There are positive reinforcements for those who toe the line and negative sanctions for those who act or behave outside the range that has been arbitrarily decided as constituting normalcy. It is imperative that females understand and appreciate their role in encouraging the way men, including HS men, choose to act and how they choose to embody masculinity.[36] Women have far more influence than they may acknowledge or understand!

Projecting

When adults feel anxious about their HSBs ability to "make it in the world" they may feel pressure, the same pressure to conform to society's dictates regarding masculinity, to instill those fears and anxieties into their HSBs. This may happen largely out of conscious awareness and, in fact, it's quite common for people to project their fears onto other people. The obvious problem here is that HSBs, like all HSPs, will absorb that fear and anxiety and make it a part of their inner world. When this happens, we set HSBs up to be fearful, to avoid taking any risks, even small ones, which only serve to confirm for the adults and HSBs that the world is too scary, too hurtful, or not worth the effort.

The reality is that we handicap HSBs when we limit them in any form! Just because a parent has experienced the world in a particular way does not mean that their perceptions, or the way they have processed them, are accurate or worthy of using as the basis for denying their boy the chance to make his own choices, for good or ill. Each boy must learn to navigate a challenging world using his own internal sense of right and wrong but can benefit from a certain amount of parental guidance early on with regards to ethics, empathy, and civility.

The French philosopher and sociologist, Edgar Morin, said, *"every human being is a cosmos, every individual swarms with virtual personalities; every psyche exudes a multitude of fantasies, dreams, and ideas."*[37] If each one of us is, indeed, a cosmos resplendent with possibilities, we should not assume that our experiences will translate into the experiences of a wholly separate person, simply because we are the parent. We should also "own" our own emotional baggage and not shift the burden onto others, this includes HSBs, who already face a challenge in learning for themselves to allow for the complexities of being highly sensitive in a largely non-highly sensitive world.

Some parents, and others, may feel uncomfortable when they spend time with an HSB who may be struggling with a particular issue of simply doing what highly sensitive people do: think, rest, observe, ask questions, etc. When deeply held pain or fears are stimulated, many people engage in a self-protective defensive posture of projecting the very qualities that they may feel about themselves but are unwilling to confront or acknowledge. We call this psychological projection and it may be quite damaging to relationships of all types.[38]

We can learn to limit our projecting by becoming aware of when we are engaging in such behaviors. We can address those deeply held feelings and work through them, so we do not simply go through life causing other people pain and suffering with inaccurate and unsupportive assessments of their character, their abilities, or their intrinsic worth as living beings. HSBs will pick up on the negative environment that is created with projection and will suffer as a result.

If we wish to encourage HSBs to become well-adjusted HS men who can embody a benevolent masculinity that avoids extreme expressions that may be so damaging to society, we have to intentionally model behaviors, thoughts, and beliefs that allow for and support differences between people. We have to find patience for our youth and invest in them while they are formative, as well as throughout life! HSBs become HS men and it is always our choice as to how we will enact culture each minute, day, week, month, and year. Culture is under constant renegotiation by each participant.

What about bullying?

The issue of bullying is a difficult topic with few good answers. Bullying occurs across all grade levels, less so in middle school. Even in the workplace, bullying is a serious issue, and little is truly effective in either punishing the bully or changing the behavior. There are some things you can do as a parent to help your HSB address bullying issues:[39]

- Choose his school wisely. The most important thing is that the educational environment is positive and supportive on average. It doesn't need to be perfect, but it does need to embody a school culture that is more positive than negative.
- Be involved in your HSBs school. Know who his teachers and counselors are and attend all parent-teacher meetings! Your child will have a better

experience if his teachers know you are involved and advocating for him.

- The school principal's commitment to anti-bullying is key to an effective policy. Zero tolerance policies are a blanket approach and fail to encompass the totality of the bullying problem. Know your principal's position on bullying and insist that it be rigorous.
- Insist on a multifaceted, comprehensive approach to bullying that addresses indirect bullying, the most common type, as well as direct bullying, less common but may be physical.

The bullying issue is not going away anytime soon. You can best help your HSB by working to ensure the policy in your child's school is indeed comprehensive and enlists all staff and faculty in the school, they have to know what to do when they see bullying or when it is reported. Effective anti-bullying policies work best when more people, including the students themselves, feel confident and empowered to do something about bad behaviors which they would otherwise feel fearful to report or reluctant to intervene in.

Should you help your HSB learn to be more assertive if he is not? What about self-defense training? Yes, it can be very helpful to help a HSB to become more assertive, to practice how he might react when he faces indirect bullying in the form of snide comments, demeaning trash talk, or intimidating and subtle inferences from bullies. Self-defense training is always a great idea, and you can do it along with your HSB! All people should know some martial arts and how to defend themselves from an attacker long enough to escape. Karate is especially good for self-defense and will build confidence in one's body and source of personal power.

I cannot emphasize enough how important it is to provide opportunities for your HSB to gain physical confidence and project at least some of it to others. Bullies often come from disadvantaged backgrounds and only understand strength. They often choose the kid who seems smaller and weaker. Don't let that kid be your HSB. Even if your HSB is a smaller child he can still learn how to project confidence. Refraining from walking alone or being alone while at school is also a proven way to minimize the chances of bullying. Bullies like to pick out the easiest prey who will not respond to their taunts. Bullies also are often deeply insecure and, later in life, go on to be more susceptible to unemployment, less achievement throughout life, and a myriad of social ills. Your HS boy may go on to quite advanced levels of education and achievement throughout life if he is well-supported. In this day and age of school shootings and heightened tension around the effects of bullying, we need to be extremely mindful of ensuring our kids are not the ones who are bullied, that appropriate interventions occur for both the bullies and the victims, and that we insist on a comprehensive anti-bullying policy at our schools.

Giftedness in highly sensitive boys

Are all HSBs gifted? Psychologist Ellen Winner described in her book, *Gifted Children: Myths and Realities* how giftedness involves three traits:

Precocity: Gifted children often demonstrate a different developmental trajectory than other children by working to master a domain sooner than other children. The domain does not matter, it is only important that the child has assimilated and integrated an entire domain long before other children have.

Creativity: Gifted children follow their own paths and discover things for themselves with very little help. This sense of curiosity is often very strong and leads the child along on his quest as a driving force. Creativity, as I have said elsewhere in this book, is for everyone at all times. No one has a lock on creativity, but gifted children exercise it to a greater degree and embrace it naturally as a way of being.

"A rage to master": Gifted children seem to follow the pattern of the flow state where the work itself is worth doing for its own sake. It is intrinsically motivating and provides a meaningful challenge to the child's abilities. He is neither overmatched to the domain or under matched. When he masters that domain or task, he has to move to the next as the same task would not provide the same intrinsic interest or rewards.

With these broad criteria in mind, it is likely that many gifted boys are indeed highly sensitive, but it should be noted that not all HS boys are gifted. Giftedness is a nebulous concept and varies to some degree in that one can master a domain yet be less competent in ordinary things such as social interactions. Giftedness can also be blocked or stunted by the boy experiencing stress, anxiety, or depressions that occupy his energies. Boys who have felt rejected or disapproved of similarly may resort to becoming people pleasers to gain acceptance and spend their energies creatively thinking of ways to fit in.

Psychologist Kazimierz Dabrowski and his theory of Positive Disintegration[40] enter the equation as well when discussing the gifted because he spent his career among the gifted and worked out his theory as a result of 30+ years of psychotherapeutic practice. Dabrowski believed that a minority of the overall population had what he thought of as overexcitabilities (OE), which he lists as:

Emotional: This OE is characterized by intense and heightened feelings, high empathy, strong attachments and deep relationships with others, and high sensitivity.

Intellectual: Intellectual OE is marked by a very active mind, strong curiosity about the world and intellectual ideas and concepts. They are usually avid readers and love to observe to seek greater understanding.

Imaginational: Children with high OE in this area often have a rich inner world where reality and fantasy are blurred and ideas flow freely. OE in this area usually entails vivid dreams, strong visual intelligence with imagery, and intense engagement with the imagination.

Sensual: The senses inform this OE as an intense experience of touch, taste, hearing, textures, smells, and seeing that leads to a heightened aesthetic in music, art, language, and that reacts strongly to unpleasant sensory stimulation.

Psychomotor: Physical action and movement typify this OE with children feeling a strong need to move their bodies, even a body part almost continuously. The surplus of static energy has to express itself through bodily movement, and energetic activity.

Dabrowski believed that one does not need to be high in all five OEs but that the most significant OEs for having high developmental potential are emotional, intellectual, and imaginational. In Dabrowski's view, high developmental potential children are most likely to be more permeable in personality with more anxieties, depressions, and a rich inner milieu that he felt was necessary for personality development at higher levels.[41]

For Dabrowski, the ones who display authentic mental health are not the rigid people who resemble a brick wall where everything simply bounces off and the wall never cracks or moves. Rather, the ones who are more permeable and who resemble a loose-stack rock wall that occasionally falls over and has to be rebuilt stronger each time. For Dabrowski, authentic mental health is exemplified through disintegrations when we lose our way for a time and come back together with a new sense of who we are and what we are about.[42]

Dabrowski's five levels of personality development allow for those with the highest levels of OEs to advance the highest over the course of a lifetime, though there is no guarantee.[43] The majority of people have some developmental potential but are typically strongly influenced and controlled by culture and its dictates.[44] High OE children would truly be those who go their own direction and pay little heed to what culture expects or demands of them. It is likely that many HS boys are high in OEs and further likely that a good number are stunted by being in "poor soil" so to speak and struggle to realize their developmental potential. Dabrowski taught that even in poor circumstances, people with high OEs would develop in place anyway, just not as well as they might in better circumstances. I was such a child.

It may seem as if many HS boys fit the criteria for either giftedness or being high in OEs, or both, but regardless, the way these children are supported needs to be similar. A positive and nurturing environment will allow the HS boy to explore on his own and develop his genius, whatever that may be, while a negative or chaotic environment will curtail or stunt his development.

Conclusion

Early support in childhood is essential to HSBs. Knowing that parents and others accept them just as they are is empowering for HSBs, who may already be quite perceptive about how they feel more deeply than others, spend more time in reflection, and feel overwhelmed at times and need to withdraw. Supporting our young boys and not bowing to cultural pressures to mold and shape our boys into the culture's vision of what a boy should be does require some courage on the part of parents but is essential in providing a firm foundation for HSBs to build on as they grow and develop.

Instead of pathologizing the supposed "weaknesses" of HSBs, we should focus on the inherent strengths they bring to our world and encourage and support them by providing rich opportunities to interact with others who are more advanced in their understandings of high potential people. Many HSBs may be quite gifted, both, as we define giftedness, and in ways that are less quantifiable and appreciated. Does high empathy make a highly sensitive boy gifted if he is able to sense when another person is suffering and lend compassionate action to that person?

Does it matter to our world when a highly sensitive boy is able to envision the world in a different way than currently exists and then works to make that a reality?

My feeling is it does matter immensely and the potential that is inherent in our HSBs is sorely needed by our societies as they become increasingly tribal, divided, egocentric and sociocentric, and less compassionate, fair, and livable. We need HSBs to grow up well so that they become well-adjusted HS men who feel comfortable in doing the work only they will do.

Questions and answers

Can we overcome early traumas in life?

It is possible to grow beyond trauma, neglect, abuse, and unsupportive environments but it does require substantial effort. Many people tend to heal and move beyond trauma to some extent as a matter of maturation and becoming parents themselves. Others find that it is through pursuing meaning in life that they can mitigate the long-term effects of early trauma. Skilled HSP-knowledgeable therapists may be a good option for those who need to begin addressing their early childhood. Later, it may be possible to do more on one's own.

My HSB is just a "strange" kid, I don't know how to feel about what he may do with himself long-term.

It's common for HSBs to be less social or to go off on their own pursuing their own interests since they are more introverted and experience non-ordinary states of consciousness more often and more readily than less sensitive people. Introversion, though, does not mean socially awkward or anxious. If your HSB is socially anxious, that is something that can be worked on over time. If he's just a "strange" kid, like I was, just be aware that he may grow up to be an incredible father, son, and paradigm-shifting HS man! Love him, support his "weirdness," his divergent way of viewing problems and approaching life and celebrate the fact that he is different in a world of sameness!

My HS boy doesn't seem to have an issue with viewing violence in movies or on television. He also doesn't necessarily avoid conflict; is this normal? What about violent video games?

All HS boys are different, just as all HS men are different. Some will avoid conflict at all costs because it is massively overstimulating, while others will not be significantly affected by viewing violence, but that may depend on exactly what he is viewing (some violence is depicted as ultra-realistic and others are obviously not harmful to the actors). There is no demonstrated link that shows that playing violent video games leads to engaging in acts of violence. If your HS boy enjoys playing these games, as long as it's in relative balance and he's not playing excessively, it's probably acceptable.

Empowerment Points

- Early childhood environment is out of our control but healing from unsupportive and non-acceptance is within our control.
- Culture is insidious in breeding conformity and parents may unconsciously push their highly sensitive boys to fit that mold regardless of potential long-term damage.

- Sensitivity may make culture less influential than self-choice.
- Mothers have a special influence over boys and should be mindful of the expectations that they communicate to their HSBs.
- We enable HS men to be well-adjusted to their wholeness through accepting and supporting who they are early on.
- Bullying is best addressed through a multifaceted and comprehensive policy at your HSBs school. Insist that they have this in place and enforce it rigorously.
- HSBs may or may not be gifted but the overall need for the early environment to be supportive and positive is the same.

CHAPTER 4

Career

"It's not what you achieve, it's what you overcome. That's what defines your career." ~Carlton Fisk

The multifaceted issue of career choice, for HS men is uniquely individual, dependent on current and future socioeconomic changes and conditions, and is always complex as we acknowledge that HS men, like all HSPs, differ widely in how they express the trait. We know that all HSPs are not alike. Other than the four D.O.E.S. core aspects of SPS, HSPs and HS men likely vary as much as in those without the trait. With that inherent diversity in mind, the problem of choosing a good career that fits well for a given individual for any period of time, will always be a moving target. Nevertheless, we will seek to address a number of salient topics that will inform and expand your view of career.

In this chapter, we will look at some of the most significant career pressures faced by men in general then apply our understanding of SPS to HS men. First, let's acknowledge that career is the most significant area of life that men feel pressure to excel in. Career carries with it many loaded implications for most of the other things that can happen in one's life such as where we live, what we live in, how we live, how long we'll live, and the quality of that life.

Considering the extreme importance that men assign to career, we also have to acknowledge the lopsided nature of that commitment, with regard to the toll that is exacted on men's physical, emotional, and mental health. When we are completely focused on one aspect of life, it becomes all too easy to become habituated to a routine and lose sight of the many other aspects of life that make life worth living for many people. Neglecting our relationships, our families, or working away in a career we are ill-matched to, but stay in because of the pressure to excel, can have devastating effects in the lives of men.

Career Choice

One of the most significant issues that HS men encounter early on is entering adult life before they have a good working understanding of their trait. They may not even be aware of SPS in any real sense or how that should inform their potential career choices. Too often, men simply choose a career that "sounds good" but fail to explore more widely or deeply enough into what it may mean to work in a given field. That lack of foresight can lead men to become stuck in career fields that they chose because they paid well or were easy to get into. Convenience is not a good metric to use when deciding on which career to choose. So, what is a good way to vet and choose an appropriate career given that HS men need to select wisely?

Over time, as I have worked with HS men, I have used the following exercise to help provide insights regarding general directions. By answering the following questions and seeing your answers visualized on paper, you can use that as a foundation on which to view prospective careers.

Questions to ask:

- What are my interests and, what do I like to do?

- What is my educational background?

- What kind of training or education would I need to acquire for a particular career?

- What are the job prospects for this career?

- Are there jobs where I live or am I able to telecommute?

- What aspects of a career matter to me the most? List your top 5 must-haves.

- What are my sensitivities? List your top 5 sensitivity concerns.

- What conditions do I need to have in place to perform at my best? List your top 3 interpersonal and environmental must-haves.

If you've engaged with this exercise deeply enough you have probably realized that a positive, supportive working environment is your paramount concern. You may have sub-points in each area, or specific concerns, but, in an overall sense it comes down to a positive and supportive working environment that is individually meaningful to you.

We know from a large survey that I conducted asking HSPs about many career issues that we can group the most popular careers into a broad helping professions category.[45] Healthcare, education, the arts, and other careers where the end result is helping people, directly or indirectly, seems to contain the highest percentage of HSPs. This is not surprising given that we need meaningful work, both to ourselves and to others. The need for meaning was one of the most cited must-haves in career for HSPs.[46] For HS men, the need for meaning in what one does for work is also paramount but may take a back seat in some regards as primacy is placed on achievement, excelling, and advancement. Men feel that they must constantly "prove" their manhood through their actions and results. In this case, it's a matter of attaining and holding status, position, and power.

The Challenge and Opportunity of Empathy

Highly sensitive men may be high in empathy, one of the four D.O.E.S. aspects of SPS. Empathy can be thought of as entering the experience of another person as if it were your own but let's unpack it further. Empathy may be thought of as cognitive, emotional, or compassionate with each type conveying advantages and disadvantages to HS men.

Cognitive empathy is intellectual in nature and means that you are able to assume the perspective of another person, but without the emotional component. Cognitive empathy may be a great advantage when we need to understand the viewpoints of others or induct new viewpoints for our own issues. Cognitive empathy is limited to the realm of the intellect but may be extremely useful in numerous instances where perspective-taking yields a better potential solution to an interpersonal, creative, or process-oriented problem.

In the same sense, when we can communicate and model what empathy looks like in action, we invite others into the experience. Cognitive empathy enhances our ability to communicate with and amongst other people as we learn to take their perspectives for a time, while working through an overall process of conveying a message. HS men may excel at cognitive empathy, since perspective taking may be a natural and easy way for SPS to demonstrate the value of noting subtleties that others overlook, employing emotional responsiveness, and putting high empathy to work in a specific way.

If cognitive empathy is a new concept to you, it is possible to cultivate this type of empathy by focusing your attention of how you may be interpreting the body language of another person. When we interpret these signals from others, we reference our own experiences, our own biases and prejudices, and what we know of the person. Exercising cognitive empathy, we are intentionally opening ourselves to the signals given off by another person, while referencing our knowledge base. We may be wrong in our judgments or interpretations and should work on tempering our often-strong intuition with prudence and patience, so we do not rush to judgement.

Allowing for our own thinking processes to enjoy time and space respects the way we HS men and all HSPs process all stimulation more elaborately. The depth of processing which we often describe takes time and patience. Reflecting on what someone has said, written, or signaled to you may take some practice as well; each person is different and will communicate in specific ways that may take some time to get to know. Be kind to yourself, and others, as you employ cognitive empathy. Model what a healthy expression looks like so that others may mimic and follow.

Contrasting with cognitive empathy is emotional empathy, the one we are all most familiar with as we enter the emotional experiences of another person and feel them as if they were our own. There is an obvious issue here for HS men with potential overstimulation as too much absorption of strong energies can overwhelm and frazzle the senses. Emotional empathy serves definite purposes in connecting us in shared experiences as we seek to relate our own experiences and feelings to another person. This process may be very informative and healing as we realize that we may not be alone in having experienced an event, thoughts, or feelings. How do we employ emotional empathy in a world that largely seems devoid and oblivious to how other people experience life?

There is a certain courage that is required with emotional empathy, along with a personal vulnerability that many people are unwilling or unable to embrace. HS men may be more willing or able to engage in emotional empathy but not if they have built up walls to keep overstimulation out to such a degree that they render themselves immune to other people's emotional experiences. Being vulnerable is not the easiest endeavor for anyone but for HS men, the task may be more difficult to some degree as they must also counter cultural conditioning of men to be stoic, emotionless, and masters of all knowledge. Men, in general, have a heavy burden placed on them to ignore the human trait of empathy, but HS men are predisposed to being well-equipped to cultivate emotional empathy as part of their trait. Emotional empathy and the resultant connections to other people on deeper levels naturally leads to our third type of empathy, compassionate empathy.

Compassionate empathy is one that I have been emphasizing for years to HSPs as the preferred result of emotional empathy. Empathy should lead us to compassionate action, in many cases. Compassion can take many forms, but HS men should resist the masculine imperative to be the "fixer" of all problems. Often, what a person in crisis needs is simply to be heard, not to have multiple solutions presented that may diminish the poignancy of the emotions felt at a given time.

Compassionate empathy may take the form of helping in a very tangible way, such as providing a ride, covering for someone who has a sick child, or helping with a complex problem. Sometimes compassionate empathy entails relating to that person what has worked for you in similar situations; however, be mindful that what worked for you will not necessarily work for another person. It is quite unpredictable how any of us may react to emotional crisis and we should be careful not to exacerbate a situation by being tone deaf, even if we feel our success may work in this case. Compassionate empathy is kind, loving, and patient. Be there for the person in a gentle way that connects, not distracts.

All three forms of empathy, in the workplace, are extremely valuable skills to cultivate and we often encounter co-workers, supervisors, and others who do not seem to understand empathy in any real sense. The opportunity is there for HS men to be the public face of empathy in all its forms. One aspect HS men should be very careful of is overstimulation.

Overstimulation

Highly sensitive men are more emotionally responsive to stimuli than men without the trait and may find themselves to feel frazzled or irritated before others might.[31] This overstimulation can come in many forms from sensory overstimulation, such as bright lights, strong smells, crowded spaces, loud talking, or any of a host of other sensitivities that are unique to each individual.[1] As one of the hallmarks of SPS, the tendency toward overstimulation, for men, is also one of the aspects many HS men wish they did not have or could mitigate.

Cultural programming instills in men that they should be unflappable in many ways. Men, according to western male culture, are expected to be stoic in the face of unpleasantness of all types and "prove" their masculinity by not reacting emotionally to stimuli. In effect, men are expected to be intentionally unemotional, even in the face of great danger.[47] Considering the overstimulation types mentioned above would hardly qualify for many men as necessitating any sort of emotional response at all; they simply would not feel that becoming overstimulated would be "manly." Derision and insults, spoken or unspoken, would likely follow for men showing strong emotion, except anger.[48] Anger would be an approved male emotion, even expected.[31]

For HS men, the problem is how to manage what may be felt quite strongly as a result of SPS, while simultaneously not appearing as a public display of any particular emotion on the surface. Many HS men report that they largely have learned to ignore most aspects of SPS except the emotional intensity component. [49] In my experiences, I find that we underestimate HS men and men without the trait as well. Men's expression of overstimulation may take the form of anger, irritation, abruptness, or mild snark but this does not mean that the stimuli are not felt, not experienced all the same; the difference is in the reactions. It also does not mean that less sensitive men do not feel or express emotion and that we should not lose sight of the oneness with which we should discuss masculinity, because it does not exist in a vacuum, nor does it exist only between men.

Let's talk about the one aspect that will drive men away from SPS faster than anything else: crying easily. It is a statistical fact borne out by numerous research studies and thousands of participants that HS men may cry more easily.[1][31][49] This does not necessarily mean they will cry but may feel emotions of such intensity that crying is the body's natural way of expressing the angst or deep nature of the stimuli. To the man who does express himself through crying when he feels intensely, we should feel in awe of his courage and authenticity as a human being to be real with his emotions. This world does not need fewer men who cry, it needs more, many more.

"Frankly, any man who doesn't cry scares me a little bit," General Norman Schwarzkopf admitted to Barbara Walters on ABC television's 20/20 program in March 1991 during the Gulf War. *"I don't think I would like a man who was incapable of enough emotion to get tears in his eyes every now and then. That person scares me; he's not a human being."*

Some of our greatest leaders cried and demonstrated that even "tough guys" cry. To cry is to express a fundamental humanity and sense of emotional intelligence that connects us to other people. We cry not because we are weak, but because we are strong. Real men cry and should never feel that their tears are shameful, unmanly, or makes them weak. True leadership is building relationships with others based on a shared humanity and acknowledging that the concerns and needs of others should be reflected back on the people whom we lead.

It is easy to paint with a broad brush and to state that overstimulation is a core aspect of SPS, but to do so without qualifying that overstimulation, specifically, what might be overstimulating, varies a great deal from man to man. It is important to emphasize this point because it is human nature to assign patterns and generalize when we should respect and acknowledge true diversity. What is overstimulating for one HS man might not affect the next at all.

There are always issues in any workplace that may prove to be overstimulating, either immediately or in the long-term. There is no one strategy to address overstimulating conditions that will work best for everyone. However, here are a few HS men might try:

Ask to dim the lights if too bright, or conversely, brighten if too dim. Note that you are not as efficient as you might be if not provided with a reasonable working environment. Use this same strategy for too hot or too cold.

Use earplugs or noise cancelling headphones to filter out extraneous noises, if allowed. There are musicians' earplugs that will quite effectively lower the volume overall without cutting down on your ability to hear others.

Unpleasant, or unpleasant for you, smells may come with the job, in some cases, but it may be possible to cut down on their intensity by asking for better ventilation or utilizing a fan. Aromatherapy oils may also help to distract the nose.

Overstimulation from loud talking, as in a cafeteria or meeting, may be unavoidable for a time. Be prepared for it in advance and know that you will need to recharge in quiet for some time afterwards.

Some situations that may prove to be overstimulating are unavoidable; we all encounter those in the workplace and we should expect it to some degree but if it is bothersome or draining for you consistently, you need to take action and try to work out a remedy. Always approach it from a value-added stance such as "I could complete this project so much more efficiently if the noise level were lower." Sometimes, you need a quiet room or a period of no noise at all so you can focus. Ask for it and do not be afraid to speak up. If possible, discuss the option of telecommuting one or more days per week. Working from home can largely mitigate overstimulation as long as your home environment is not similarly chaotic or overstimulating!

Need for Meaning

HS men, because they process all stimuli in a more elaborate way, tend to strongly prefer work that has real meaning. This makes sense when we consider the amount of time and energy expended on the thinking, reflecting, and processing of all stimuli. Meaningful work potentially equals a better use of rational and creative abilities and capacities. Less meaningful work, or work that is excessively repetitious or boring, is not as well suited to the unique capabilities of the HS man.

The need for meaning can best be conceptualized through Self-Determination Theory (SDT): a theory of human motivation based on the central concept of intention. SDT distinguishes between extrinsic and intrinsic motivation with intrinsic motivation as the preferred factor because, when a person is motivated to work toward a goal that is meaningful and important in a personal sense, he will derive personal benefits in the form of increased self-esteem, greater self-confidence, and mastery over a given domain.[50] He will also enjoy the work because it is self-directed.

Extrinsic motivation, by contrast, is brought on from outside the individual in the form of rewards of one sort or another: high grades, more money, prestige, high praise from others, or as a desire to avoid a punishment for not achieving a task. Both forms of motivation are useful, but only intrinsic motivation is worth doing for its own sake. When an activity is autonomously chosen, we enjoy the experience of achieving the goal. This is especially true for HS men, who benefit more from positive environments, due to Vantage Sensitivity.

We mentioned autonomy here and we should expand on this because autonomy is one of the most often cited aspects of career that sensitive people tend to mention as important for them.[46] Whether it's having the freedom to choose the goal or task or deciding how to carry out how to achieve the goal, HS men do better when they are able to work in autonomous conditions. This does not mean that they do not necessarily work well within a structure; indeed, some HS men might prefer a structure to minimize anxieties about unknowns. Others prefer the freedom to work autonomously, especially if they are also high in sensation seeking and require frequent novelty.[51]

The Quiet Leader: Leading with Sensitivity

Leaders are often envisaged as loud, demanding, and aggressive but that is an outdated notion that largely does not hold true in the modern workplace where emotional intelligence is valued as a means to, fundamentally, make work happen by creating an environment where people feel valued, supported, and aligned with the values of the company. It's often been said that a company's culture starts "at the top" and it's never truer than when leadership comes into focus.

Highly sensitive men may make terrific leaders because they are naturally empathetic, meaning they are able to sense the affective and emotional states of other people. This ability exists at a high level for highly sensitive men and enables them to feel when things seem "off," or when another person is hurting or becoming upset. Empathy in the HS man, and leader, is a huge asset as interpersonal issues need to be navigated, mitigated, and resolved to, not only keep the peace, but to enable a flourishing working environment.

Men who are highly sensitive will notice subtleties that others may overlook. The ability to pick up on subtle details or cues may be a deciding factor in interpersonal interactions, but also in creativity and innovation, where divergent thinking inducts many new ideas and convergent thinking assesses those ideas or concepts. Subtle connections or nuances may be more apparent to the HS man, and he may be the only member of a team to avoid the all too human tendency toward groupthink, simply because he senses the details around the edges that others miss.

Couple high empathy with sensitivity to subtleties and a deep reflective capacity and you have a formidable combination! Leaders in the modern age need to embody these personal qualities and be able to apply them to a multitude of work situations and circumstances that may be quite complex, dynamic, and ambiguous. The HS man as a leader may be quite varied in demeanor, because all HS men are not the same and differ widely in how they might express the trait, but will typically be high in emotional intelligence. So, what do we mean by the "quiet leader?"

Quiet leadership is about allowing employees to shine and not the leader.[52] Quiet leaders tend to eschew the limelight and do not seek accolades for themselves, instead preferring to let the employees gain confidence as they grow and develop. Quiet leadership is rooted in the concept of servant leadership where the ego is largely set aside and one views leading others as a supporting and nurturing role rather than a controlling, demanding one.[53] Servant leaders, though the term may seem to imply subordination, are anything but subordinate.[54]

The true servant leader knows that you get the best out of your employees and team members by taking an interest in facilitating their growth and development, by supporting and encouraging their talents and abilities, and by being the kind of leader who inspires rather than cajoles or intimidates.[55] The HS man who is a servant leader may embody leadership in this "quieter" way that places the focus on his teams and employees.[53]

The quiet leader may be highly emotionally intelligent and intensely attuned to the people who work for him.[56] There has been much written about introverted leaders and how they may be better listeners, comfortable with solitude, better planners, better problem solvers because they challenge their own notions and dig deep into complex problems, while remaining calm and steady, even when others are excitable or upset. The HS leader will likely be introverted, owing to about 70% of HSPs overall being introverted, but being highly sensitive will distinguish him from introverts in important ways like processing ideas and concepts very deeply, possessing a broader range of possible emotional responses, noticing subtle cues like sounds, visual distinctions, strong empathy that connects them to other people innately, and a general sensitivity in all situations.

We must also acknowledge that not all HS men are introverts. About 30% are extraverted and may be anything but quiet.[1] The extraverted HS leader may seem like any other extravert, at first glance, but being highly sensitive does mean that he will likely tire of lengthy interactions or fatigue in demanding energetic circumstances. He shares that with any HSP in that they all need to recharge in quiet throughout the day. Extraverted HS leaders may do very well in leading more passive employees, likely including introverted HSPs on his team.

The quiet leader isn't interested in materialism or finding happiness and equality through purely economic means. Indeed, the quiet leader has a sense of moral imperative to care for others while growing their potential. The quiet leader is more of a shepherd than a wolf and patiently guides his flock towards success through kindness, empathy, and a greatly lessened ego than is typical in leadership positions. A quiet leader does well in many leadership roles but there is a place for brash leadership as well. For example, it's been noted that

Apple's co-founder, Steve Jobs, was quite insistent and demanding as a leader and perhaps that was what was needed during that phase of their history, but Tim Cook, the current CEO is more low-key, which seems to be more in tune with Apple's status and level of employees that they are able to attract and retain now.

Self-Employment

With the many challenges HS men face in choosing and sustaining a career for the long-term, self-employment enters the picture as a viable alternative to expending incredible amounts of time and energy to fit one's working life around dysfunctional workplace cultures. Many HS men have simply "had enough" of the corporate world and wish to do something that is, not only different, but potentially offers greater flexibility in how work is arranged and performed, the types of people one chooses to work with (customers, clients, and co-workers), and, ultimately, the direction and pace of one's life. There is no greater equalizer that I am aware of, or believe in as much, than working for oneself.

I have written about self-employment before in my earlier book on career[45] and felt that communicating a certain amount of caution was appropriate at that time because venturing out onto one's own can be a scary time for an HSP. Over the past few years, as I have watched the economy change with the rise of online business opportunities, freelancing made easier by websites like Fiverr and Upwork, and a range of new business ideas stemming from shifts in society around how we use technology to shop, pay for things, and utilize services, self-employment is not only not as scary as it was years ago, it is becoming the norm! In 2020, as I write this book, the pandemic of the Corona Virus has dramatically shown us how it is quite feasible to have much of our workforce working from home.

For some HS men who have been forced to work at home, I am sure they can now see the advantages and disadvantages of living and working in one space. Some will prefer to return to an external environment, but the high performers will likely much prefer the home environment if it provides them with time and space to think, focus, and work distraction-free.[57]

The Con in Independent Contracting

We should qualify here that self-employment is also being used loosely by society to describe workers forced to work as independent contractors. Such work has its advantages and disadvantages and entails all of the same risks and responsibilities of operating a business. For example, as a contractor, you must pay all of your own income taxes, you may be responsible for providing your insurance, and you have to use your own personal vehicle, depending on the work.

My story

I worked years ago as an independent contractor for one of the largest distributors of fresh tortillas in the US, and beyond. I provided my own vehicle, a large cargo van that I purchased, my own warehouse, to hold my weekly deliveries of products, and I paid for all of my business expenses related to working as a distributor. Since I lived in a fairly rural area, I had to drive quite a lot to reach my customers, who were primarily the large grocery stores in surrounding towns, as well as the smaller grocers and restaurants. Yes, I made reasonable money, but it was also a seven day a week task to take care of everything and every account that I had.

The particular company whom I was contracted with, a contract that highly favored them in all instances, was, in many instances, unreliable and hard to work with in such mundane things as being paid on time. My weekly checks made it possible to have gas to run the route each week and when checks were late, sometimes by many weeks, it meant my family was poor and we lived at a minimal level until things were straightened out.

Similarly, with the business model, I was forced to "purchase" the product and, if it did not sell, it was my problem. Fresh tortillas, by the way, have a short shelf life, like fresh bread and when sales were inexplicably slow, I suffered the losses. Some good did come of it in that I arranged to donate unsold tortillas, still edible mind you, to our local Salvation Army food pantry, who then distributed them to the needy.

The route I "owned" was in very bad shape when I assumed it with grocery managers who were very off put by the previous four distributors, in the past year, who had all abandoned ship when they lost money. I stuck with it and built a reputation over several years of punctuality, good service, and well-kept displays in my stores. I eventually paid people to restock some items on weekends in my far-flung areas so that I could cut back on the mileage I was burdened with driving. This worked, overall, for a period of time.

The regional supervisor, whom I had had a reasonable working relationship with, was eventually replaced and the new guy was a fairly unreasonable, unhinged, angry sort of person who became incredibly difficult to work with. This person had a reputation for incompetence within the company, so I knew that as he came in, that this situation was in jeopardy. I determined to sell off the route and gain my small profit from several years of built-up good will and had a buyer within days of closing when the new supervisor decided to invent a problem that would allow them to literally take the route back with no compensation on my part. Frankly, by that point, I was relieved to be rid of the burden that it had become but, obviously, not happy about the outcome.

I relate this story from my long history of holding bad jobs to illustrate that independent contracting "opportunities" may be just as much or more of a pain than regular employment, with more risk on your part. Think carefully before taking on such relationships, such arrangements are becoming the norm in much of the US economy. In my view, if you're going to be taking all the risk and potentially suffering the consequences, of contracting, you might as well work for yourself in your own small business. Why participate in what is typically a one-sided relationship when the deck is always stacked against you?

What I Learned

Over the years I have worked in a number of ill-suited, from an HSPs perspective, jobs and positions. My options were greatly limited by two factors: I was not as self-aware then about SPS and did not have a full understanding of how deeply it influenced my needs, and because for a large portion of my adult life, I lived in a small city, meaningful employment opportunities were scarce. When we have spent many years playing the societal game of working hard, doing our best to fit in, and it is obvious that to continue attempting to shoehorn ourselves into a role that simply does not fit us, we are left to either continue suffering or find a different way. I chose a different way.

It might be correctly stated that I always approached adult life with an entrepreneurial orientation and knew intuitively that I functioned better on my own. I spent my very early years as a young adult as a member of the US Army. I was an air defense missile crewman on a HAWK anti-aircraft system in Germany during the mid-1980s during the late Cold War period. Not what you might expect from an HSP, but I was desperate to escape small town Missouri!

As my first real job, the Army taught me many things and afforded me the chance to learn about myself. I learned that I prefer to work alone or with just a few people, as part of a small, highly proficient team. I learned that I could be very good at very hard tasks and, in fact, excel. I learned that my future would certainly not be a military career – simply too boring and, for me, depressing – and that my path would be one of exploration and change.

Small business always appealed to me, just intrinsically, because for the guy who has a real problem with authority figures – replete in many workplaces – running one's own business removed this source of contention, stress, and anxiety. I did work for a few leaders or managers who were good at taking care of their team members but, by and large, I did not find that to be the norm. Self-employment put me in charge and afforded me the opportunity to operate in such a way as to minimize confrontation, enjoy autonomy, and be in creative control of my venture.

Over the years, I tried many business-related ventures such as delivering newspapers in rural areas via car, growing Shiitake mushrooms, landscaping, and the sales route previously mentioned. I learned from each of these concepts and continually bear those lessons in mind and you will as well.

Small business is the great equalizer. It seems that we quite often hear about new startups seeking funding through Kickstarter or that "XYZ" company has invented a new app, but what we do not usually hear about are all the small home-owned and operated small businesses started and run by entrepreneurs. Often it is single moms or people who have been displaced from the workforce in some way that decide to go into business for themselves and take their chances on their own leadership and hard work. Small business affords us the opportunity to find an idea, develop it, and build a business around it.

When you work for yourself, there are pluses and minuses, but the pluses usually outweigh the minuses. Yes, you are assuming all of the risk and will suffer with a bad idea or badly executed idea but the lesson there is do your homework, know your market, and never stop learning.

Career is one of the most significant areas of life that HS men feel pressured in to deliver the goods in terms of achievement, advancement, and stability. This sense of extreme pressure takes a toll on HS men in exhaustion, stress, and, ultimately, burnout. Burnout is simultaneously a good reason to think about self-employment and not such a good reason. The new possibilities in self-employment may solve many of the problems that led to the feelings of burnout but entering a demanding new chapter of life while feeling depleted will not exactly breed enthusiasm for the new venture.

I always advise HS men to consider starting their business as a side business that they can build while remaining employed. The side "gig" as it now seems to be called, is a great way to make the current situation more bearable, at least for a while, and possibly provide new and needed stimulation. If you are also a high sensation seeker as well as an HSP, the need for novelty and new experiences is likely to be undeniable.

"One of the huge mistakes people make is that they try to force an interest on themselves. You don't choose your passions; your passions choose you." -Jeff Bezos, Amazon founder

Finding Your Way

Career is the biggest area of life that HS men feel pressured in to perform and achieve. Modern masculinity, as it is commonly embodied, is immensely stressful and anxiety-producing in requiring men to continually prove their manhood by continual achievement, domination, and aggression. All are unhealthy when taken to extremes and men, in general, suffer greatly throughout their life course with depression, unspoken anxiety, PTSD, and other signs of a stressed organism but are unable to reach out for help for fear of being seen as weak.

If being seen as weak is our deepest fear and exists in us to such a degree that it drives us to extreme behavior in ways that are incompatible with our true nature, we have truly lost our way as human beings. If, instead, we choose to live our lives from a standpoint of personal authenticity, without regard for judgements from society, we fall in line with our natural flow and energies.

The ability to adapt our lives economically is why I'm so excited to advocate for self-employment for many HS men! There are numerous ways that exist now to use the internet, and the many companies now with deep ties to internet commerce, to build your own business and escape the desperate trap of working for the corporations and organizations that have failed to offer positive and supportive working environments.

Finding your way as a HS man will never be easy and career is likely to be one of your most significant challenge areas in this lifetime. Self-employment and entrepreneurship are not the only avenues in which a HS man may find success. HS men work in all career fields and are not limited any more than anyone else might be. The only difference is HS men, if they subscribe to societal notions of what constitutes a man, will suffer if they are not able to live up to that standard. That negativity will, in turn, deeply affect the HS man's life as we know from Vantage Sensitivity.

It is also not likely that you will find that your life will follow a strict linear trajectory without twists and turns, attempts and failures, detours and divergences. It is perfectly normal for a HS man, who is, after all, a complex human being, to expect that finding the best fit will take some time. Perhaps it is best to think of career as an ever-evolving construct rather than a singular event because the modern world often does not allow for one choice in career without the pace of change overtaking the viability of a particular career field. HS men should expect that it will take some experimentation, which involves risk and failure at times, before they arrive at concepts and ideas that actually fit them well. They should also expect that that good fit will change as they change, and career switches will likely be a normal fact of life.

If you are a HS man with deep anxiety or from an unsupportive childhood, you should know that it is still possible to find security and predictability in career, if that is what you value the most. There will always be positions that are necessary to the smooth functioning of society and should remain fairly stable over time. Even within careers that hold less movement one can still find solid income, reasonable work, and a pleasant enough working environment. Those types of positions can be found in any community but, of course, will depend on persistence, connections, and qualifications to attain them.

If you are already successful in your career, I would not be surprised, knowing how talented many HS men are but if you haven't found a career that works for you, I would also not be surprised, knowing how incredibly difficult it can be. My advice to you in finding your way is to search for the best positive and supportive environment you can find, it doesn't need to be 100% supportive, just on average. If you cannot find the environment that you need, you may need to create it for yourself. In my view, you are well-suited to the type of research and planning that goes into creating a small business and you will likely be quite adept at applying your conscientious nature – the only proven correlate to workplace performance – to your business concept.

What about high sensation seeking HS men? Are there careers that work well for them? The HSS/HS man is a unique blend of the need to continually push forward while simultaneously pumping the brakes slightly to avoid taking undue risks. HSS/HS men are highly creative, driven by a need to reinvent themselves and experience new people, situations, and stimulation. They do not do well in repetitive or dull environments. For this reason, HSS/HS men may do best with relatively short-term projects where they know a definite ending date and have autonomy in how to get the job done.[51]

High sensation seeking HS men are not driven solely by sensation seeking. They are counterbalanced by the need to reflect and to consider their plans before acting on thoughts and ideas. Nevertheless, the HSS/HS man is unlike any other man in that he experiences what can only be described as a drive to create, to experience, and to live. HSS/HS men may combine the best of both worlds if they are able to be self-aware enough to understand and balance both traits.

This same drive will compel the HSS/HS man to push through fear to achieve his goals, which can be very good for the sensitive side. Often high sensitivity is a cautionary instinct that may become so involved in turning over the nuances of a problem to ever move into action. Sensation seeking and its implicit drive to reinvent and experience will push the HSS/HS man out of his comfort zone and towards his goals.

HSS/HS men may make ideal entrepreneurs, creatives of all kinds, and skilled tradespeople. The HSS/HS man will thrive on the flow experience and waste away without it. One trap to watch out for: the HSS/HS man may become enamored of a new idea and be highly enthused for a time, even spending a great deal of time and effort in research. He will absorb everything there is to know about a topic and become a near-expert only to lose interest if things do not move along quickly enough. I call these "fascinations" and every HSS/HS man will, I know, be able to relate to that term.[51] There is a positive side to accumulating so much specific knowledge on various topics and forgoing them later: he becomes a very well-rounded person with detailed knowledge to draw on in the future. Combine that with the deep mind, kind heart, and sensitivity to all things so endemic to HSPs and you have a formidable pairing of traits!

Surviving among the "Alpha Males" in the Corporate World

What if you are already deeply invested in a career in the corporate world and find yourself surrounded by Alpha male types? In the Myth of the Alpha Male, by humanistic psychologist Scott Barry Kaufman, we gain a new perspective on what is a limiting perspective on masculinity.[58] Alpha males, or at least the stereotype of the alpha male, is at the top of social hierarchy and got there through domination, intimidation, and physical presence. Beta males, by contract, are thought of as weak, subordinate and of low status. Both are a limited and inaccurate viewpoint that poses only two paths for men to emulate.

Kaufman details how dominance can take many forms. For example, the dominant male who is "demanding, violent, and self-centered is not considered attractive to most women, whereas the dominant male who is assertive and confident is considered attractive."[58] Further research suggests that sensitivity and assertiveness are not opposites. Combining kindness with assertiveness seemed to represent the most attractive coupling of traits to potential mates.

It seems that pro-social behaviors, when combined with achievement-oriented behaviors, such as conscientiousness, agreeableness, empathy, and genuine self-esteem yield social prestige that may be viewed as higher social status. One can take the dominance route to social status, but HS men are not likely to be aggressive, to intimidate others, or to create an environment for themselves or others that is unsupportive. We know this from Vantage Sensitivity where it has been well established that sensitive people do worse than average in unsupportive or negative environments and better than average in supportive and positive environments.[3]

Applying this to the corporate office, if you are the quiet leader who has a higher social status built on attaining prestige and not dominance, you are already the "alpha male" in this situation. The stereotype of the alpha male would be woefully ill-equipped to lead unless he were in the harshest circumstances where aggression and intimidation would allow him to achieve a desperate goal. The quiet leader, by contrast, is best equipped to lead in most other circumstances where people are less inclined to submit to an impulsive and rash expression of masculinity.

In the corporate world, if you choose to take on the stress of office politics and drama, you will need to bear a few things in mind:

Leaders who choose to intimidate and coerce will always be present.

Leaders who choose to lead by aggression and dominance generally do not care about focusing on creating a positive working environment.

Attaining high social status through gaining prestige places you in the actual alpha position.

Your power is likely far greater in helping your company reach its goals because it inspires others to invest themselves in the work rather than to tolerate it.

Highly sensitive men who have attained high social status through gaining social prestige, not at all uncommon, are in a better position to influence and empower others in performing at their best. The quiet leader, as I like to describe the HS man, is by nature a more pro-social leader capable of creating and sustaining working environments where people feel heard, seen, and valued. Some HS men may need to work on their assertiveness, confidence, and embodiment of social prestige in order to be known for their true potential. Too often, we are overlooked because we are easygoing or prefer to be absorbed in our work rather than to be the center of attention.

Learning to find a comfort level with public speaking or standing in the limelight may not be easy for you, but it is entirely possible. My advice is to work on this a little bit at a time by doing small things to build social skills and confidence. For example, you might choose to volunteer as a coach for your kid's sports team. I did so and it was a great way to step into a more public role, while doing something meaningful. I found that I spent more time developing my players than did other coaches and witnessed amazing growth in my young athletes! That experience, along with similar experiences, started to build a sense of confidence that grew over the years as I continued to "step up" and say yes to opportunities that came my way, but which may have mildly terrified me inside.

Yes, learning to speak up is hard. We HS men usually do not enjoy the feeling of all eyes on us or being judged, especially if we suffered shame, ACEs in childhood, or were simply never mentored by anyone. One of the best things you can do for yourself is to do what you do best: observe others and think about how you might emulate some of their pro-social behaviors and tactics. Think about asking someone who has higher social status based on prestige to serve as your mentor, it's likely that yes will be the answer, given that's how they attained their status! You can't get what you don't ask for.

Once you have built up your confidence and status, it will then be a matter of using sound judgement to understand the importance of timing and when to insert yourself to maximum effect. The quiet leader understands when to let the boisterous leaders have their say and when to be the one in the limelight. Make no mistake, your quiet leadership is desperately needed in the corporate world! Work to build your social influence so you can wield it in ways that complement and enhance your company's goals, while allowing you to embody the kind of quiet leadership that builds and sustains cooperation, mentoring, and positive working environments.

Questions and answers

What's the best career for a HS man?

This is a uniquely individual situation and there are many variables that will determine career fit for any one HS man. The "helping" professions seem to statistically employ the largest segment of the HSP population. However, HS men are not limited in any way, but they must consider how well a career fits them rather than attempting to fit themselves into a career that is obviously wrong for them. HS men tend to stay in wrong fits for too long and should continually consider how to best adapt their lives to fit their needs throughout the life course. HS men may do fine in any career field and already are, in fact, in a wide variety of possible careers.

Empowerment Points

- Career choice is complex for HS men and should ideally occur with a high level of self-awareness to avoid being in an ill-suited career.
- The development of compassionate empathy in HS men makes us well-suited to careers in the helping professions.
- Overstimulation is highly individual in HS men. One should be aware of one's trigger stimuli and choose a career that is suited, on the average, to a need to avoid too much overstimulation.

CHAPTER 5

Perceptions are Not What They Seem

"Our life always expresses the result of our dominant thoughts." ~Soren Kierkegaard

Highly sensitive men may feel as if they are perceived in a negative way by others in society but to a large extent, they may pay more attention to the perceptions of others than is warranted. The perceptions of others may be quite faulty, and our own perceptions may be unduly influenced by our overflowing thoughts. In this chapter, we will discuss how the way that we perceive reality may be distorted by our own inner critical processes and how we can reframe perceptions to reflect a more accurate representation of reality.

HS men may be acutely focused on what they have come to believe are their deficiencies, but which are not undesirable qualities at all for any human being. Being told that there is "something wrong with you," that you need to "toughen up," or that "you're not a REAL man unless you do this" communicates to the HS boy that his core essence as a person is unacceptable and, in some cases, despised. When a HS boy grows up to be a HS man and perceives that others also possess similar views of his worth or character, he may come to believe it himself.

Perceptions are the views that we hold to be true and accurate about the world. The way we develop these beliefs is deeply influenced by numerous factors such as social class, education level, and early childhood environment. HS men, like all HSPs, are naturally predisposed to reflect on events that occur throughout life to a greater degree than in those who are less sensitive. This greater quantity of processing doesn't mean that we are able to arrive at beliefs in an accurate way. Often, we subscribe to faulty beliefs without being aware of it. These faulty perceptions contribute to who we think we are, for better or worse. Many HS men have experienced some degree of negative associations with being sensitive and, as a result, are likely to have developed faulty perceptions that may last a lifetime.

There are a couple of main points that are important for HS men to know regarding perceptions and how to challenge them:

1) Confirmation bias implies that we tend to subscribe to a belief and look for information that supports our position while ignoring all information that supports an opposing position. That is most evident today in the deep political polarization in the US.

   To effectively refute confirmation bias, we apply our critical thinking skills, which asks us to consider the information we are using, assumptions we may be making, and the questions being asked. If we can find objectivity where formerly there was subjectivity, it will go a long way toward minimizing confirmation bias in our thinking.

2) We make assumptions by lumping like things together and assuming all will exhibit the same actions and behaviors. For example, perhaps you had a less sensitive person make a less than flattering comment about how quiet you are. You might assume that another similar person would

think and act in the same way but that would be to deny the plasticity we humans embody.

Grouping things together may be a convenient way to quickly develop a context for like things but may be grossly inaccurate. To challenge this tendency, remain open to the fact that all people are different and may act and react differently in various situations and circumstances. To assign homogenous qualities to similar people is like saying all HS men are alike, which is patently untrue.

3) The anchoring effect links us to false beliefs of value. In essence, the anchoring effect establishes what may be a false baseline from which you may rank everything else. For example, a negative experience with a new situation might anchor us at a low point, but not all similar experiences will be negative.

4) Our perceptions are dependent on our moods. If we are feeling depressed or anxious it's likely that our perceptions are reflecting the moment and will change later as our mood changes. For example, when we are in a low mood, our perceptions may reflect the same energy and conversely when we are in a high mood, our perceptions may be quite different.

There is a commonality here that I hope you can pick up: we make faulty initial perceptions then expect future situations to result in the same results. Anchoring at a low point is obviously setting our expectations too low, while anchoring at a high point will set us up for disappointment if expectations are not met.   The best anchor is the moderately optimistic one that allows for possibilities.

Similar to this concept is positive psychologist Martin Seligman's flexible optimism, which tempers optimism with a modest pessimism.[59] Pessimism can be very useful in preventing us from being overly optimistic when we should be skeptical. A flexible optimism provides us with a healthy dose of skepticism that continually calls into question our perceptions.

The Dreaded Inner Critic

Highly sensitive men have a strong built-in inner critic, by which I mean a tendency to harshly criticize ourselves due to poor actions, words, thoughts, or intentions that we may have. We are the hardest on ourselves! We also tend to take negative criticism directly to heart and may be deeply affected by it to an undue extent. When we become self-criticizers, we also become highly defensive and will retreat from the things that hurt us. This is obviously a problem when we consider that our actions are almost always being judged by someone at some point.

The harsh inner critic may influence the way we view the world or each other.[60] Someone criticizes you and you may find yourself swearing off that person for life! Of course, one of the problems is most people are not very good at providing either feedback or criticism and go about it by pointing out a deficiency only. There are a couple of points about giving and receiving criticism or feedback that are important for HS men to learn:

- When providing feedback or criticism to others, ensure that you say several respectful and decent things about that person's performance before the negative feedback. That primes the person with proportionally more good observations than bad and will soften what may be otherwise received poorly.

- Feedback should always be timely, specific, and actionable. Don't wait until months later to drop feedback on someone's performance, do it soon after the problem is noted so it's fresh in the person's mind. Likewise, make your feedback highly specific, while noting exactly what they did right or wrong and exactly how they might improve. Never just generally criticize ambiguously without specificity. Lastly, feedback should always include how the person might improve his performance. Never leave it at "you did A, B, and C incorrectly," always provide the resources the person may need to improve. Sometimes he may need more training or mentoring to learn how to improve. Be patient with others and provide encouragement as he improves.

- When receiving criticism, first, understand that criticism should never be directed at you personally. Criticism can never be a positive force if you are being demeaned or devalued as a person. It is fair to critique a man's performance or behaviors but not his character or sense of worth.

- You will likely overreact to all negative criticism, running the words of the other person over and over in your mind for what seems to be an eternity. That is natural for HS men and is a benefit when we consider that evolution favors those who are able to learn how to navigate the rough waters of interpersonal interactions. We are a highly social species and learn throughout the life course how to communicate with each other. Know that the strong feelings will pass, it may take a day, but they will pass, and you will feel differently when you are able to think rationally.

- Question your inner critic as he harshly berates you for not reacting appropriately, becoming upset (even feeling upset), or for not "getting over it" quickly enough. Seligman asks us to question negative thoughts by engaging the three P's: ask yourself whether the situation is permanent, pervasive, or personal.[59]

By permanent, I mean will the feeling last forever or will it pass? Is the situation permanent or is it a one-time bit of feedback? In most cases, criticisms or feedback, I much prefer the term feedback for its positive tone, are one-time events and not a daily occurrence.

Pervasive implies that what you're feeling will affect everything in your life. Often, we can discount feedback as affecting everything and see it for its intended effect, which is usually to help us improve. Feedback should always be viewed as specific and local to a single situation.

As we discussed earlier, feedback should never be personal, and you should never accept personal criticism when directed at you as a human being. The inner critic will tell you that you're unintelligent, not quick enough, or not a good person, but those are easy to refute when you examine your life overall.

You know within yourself that you are a good man, that you work hard, or that you can do anything you take on, never doubt that.

The inner critic is multiplied in HS men and must be tamed to some extent if we are to truly embody a confidence in the world that allows us to realize our potential. Many of us are quite used to entering that internal running dialog that tells us we can't do something or that we're not good enough. For those of us who were highly criticized in our early years, the power of the inner critic is magnified, and we may not understand how damaging it is when it may be all we have ever known. Most of us tend to grow beyond intense self-criticism as a result of maturing over the life course and encountering numerous obstacles as adults, parents, and participants in the modern workforce.

Depending on where you are in age you may require some professional assistance with taming the inner critic. Therapy can certainly help but be very careful to work with an HSP-knowledgeable professional. You can find a list of HSP-knowledgeable therapists at Dr. Aron's website at https://hsperson.com/therapists/seeking-an-hsp-knowledgeable-therapist/. It can also be quite helpful to engage in what is called post-processing with a trusted friend or mentor. Post processing is exactly what it sounds like and provides an objective view of what you are perceiving and feeling. Often, having someone else who can tell us that what we're thinking is accurate and rational helps to contextualize the swirling thoughts and feelings. Seek out someone who is patient, objective, and who practices rational thinking; yes, it is a lifelong practice we should all engage in.

Social Anxiety

Many HS men have a lingering perception that something is "wrong with them" and that sooner or later they will be found out and exposed to shame or embarrassment. Social anxiety is a fear of negative social sanction for perceived flaws, deficiencies, or a feeling that who we are fundamentally is not good enough. According to clinical psychologist Ellen Hendrikson, who wrote the book, How To Be Yourself: How to Quiet Your Inner Critic and Rise Above Social Anxiety, social anxiety is a "package deal that often comes bundled with strengths like high standards and empathy and being helpful and altruistic.[61] People who have social anxiety are often good listeners and conscientious and they work hard to get along with fellow humans." In this view, social anxiety is a faulty perception on our parts that can be changed.

Hendrikson suggests that we develop confidence by placing action before mood, meaning we build confidence as a result of doing a challenging task. For example, if there is a social event a HS man might like to attend, but he feels anxious about the crowd that will inevitably be there, he may overthink it and may wind up not going at all! But if he pushed through his fear and attended anyway, he may well find that his mood is quite different after having overcome a personal challenge. He may also feel greater confidence at the next social event and less fear of social rejection.

As a lifelong socially anxious HS man, I can attest to the efficacy of placing action before mood. In my life, I have only ever built personal confidence as a result of pushing myself to do the things that scared me; social events and public speaking of all kinds being chief among them. Hendrikson describes anticipatory anxiety as the initial anxiety we feel so strongly prior to a social interaction. She advocates for "being brave for one minute" with the knowledge that anxiety tends to level off after the one-minute mark and we feel less anxious as the moments pass.

Many of us have developed safety behaviors which we can retreat to such as checking our phones or retreating to safe places in a room, usually the edges, as we seek anywhere that will feel less threatening. Hendrikson advises that indulging in safety behaviors can hamper our progress toward relaxed and unforced interactions that have a natural flow. It does take courage and a willingness to put ourselves "out there" but the sense of confidence can be life changing!

Learning to minimize our social anxiety takes real effort and will not happen overnight since social anxiety is a learned behavior. Reframing our core self attributes as fundamentally positive and worthwhile can help to change faulty perceptions. As you may notice, improving ourselves often involves engaging with our rational thinking capabilities to challenge and refute faulty perceptions and beliefs about ourselves.

Psychological Androgyny and the HS Man

There is another aspect of our disposition as sensitive men that directly influences how we perceive the world: the concept of psychological androgyny. Here, I am referring to psychologist Mihaly Csikszentmihalyi's version of androgyny to describe a much wider concept. In Csikszentmihalyi's view, one can be psychologically androgynous by simultaneously embodying what seem like opposite poles such as aggressive and nurturant, dominant and submissive, or rigid and sensitive, regardless of gender.[62]

Bear in mind, that we imply a psychological androgyny here, not a sexual one. It is well-known that sensitive people are more emotionally responsive. In fact, emotional responsiveness is one of the four core aspects of SPS, meaning we interact with the world in a much richer and more varied way based on our broader range of emotional depth and breadth. Csikszentmihalyi said that the one word that can best describe a creative person is complexity. Complexity applies equally to HS men in that we rarely feel one emotion at a time, unless it is anger. A HS man effectively doubles his range of possible responses but living with this complexity requires a commiserate ability to filter and contextualize all of the thoughts, feelings, and possibilities.

Rational Thinking and the HS Man

There is an effective way to refute our own perceptions that can cross-pollinate other areas of our lives: critical thinking. Critical thinking means to discern using criteria, in this case, I will refer to the model advocated by Richard Paul and Linda Elder.[63] The core essence of the approach utilizes universal elements of reasoning that are assessed and evaluated by universal standards of thinking to reason our way through complex problems. Note that we don't need to engage this process to the full extent on mundane issues of everyday life but when we are facing the swirling thoughts, feelings, and emotions we HS men know so well the Paul-Elder model can help us to ferret out our bias's and assumptions that may be leading us to faulty perceptions.

The universal elements of reasoning are:

- All reasoning has a purpose
- All reasoning is an attempt to figure something out, to settle some question, to solve some problem
- All reasoning is based on assumptions
- All reasoning is done from a point of view
- All reasoning is based on data, information, and evidence
- All reasoning is expressed through, and shaped by, concepts and ideas
- All reasoning contains inferences and interpretations by which we draw conclusions and give meaning to data
- All reasoning leads somewhere or has implications and consequences

Anyone can easily use this set of elements to reason with by working to understand one by one what is being considered in each case. For example, clearly understanding our purpose is crucial to knowing why we are thinking in the first place. All thinking is an effort to understand something, to work out a solution to a problem. We don't think for the sake of thinking, we think to solve a problem. The more we know about the problem under consideration, by using these elements of reasoning, the greater the context we have to reason with.

While we are working through the elements of reasoning on a problem, we should apply a quality checking set of standards to assess the level of our thought. We call these the universal standards of thinking and they are easily remembered and used anytime we need to think, speak, listen, or write. The standards of thinking are:

- Clarity
- Accuracy
- Precision
- Relevance
- Significance
- Depth
- Breadth
- Logic
- Fairness

We use these standards as a way of testing our thinking, speaking, writing, and listening. The standards may also be applied to the thinking, speaking, writing, and listening of other people. That is: we can assess our own thinking and the thinking of others using the standards. For HS men, we can use either the standards alone as a way to question our perceptions and the thinking that is inherent in it, or use the standards in conjunction with the elements of reasoning as a way to work through complex issues. We may often believe that we are thinking rationally but when you try applying the elements to your thinking, you will quickly see how little you actually understand about the nature of the problem you are consumed with.

HS men may feel overwhelmed by the sheer volume of thoughts and feelings that can occupy our minds when encountering a real problem. Learning to use the Paul-

Elder approach to critical thinking will help to discipline your thinking and improve your ability to think rationally.

Questions and answers

I feel like all eyes are on me in public spaces, how can I challenge this perception?

This is a common feeling among HS men as we tend to be acutely self-aware. Unless you are wearing very colorful clothes or calling attention to yourself in some way, it is not likely that others are actually watching you. Often people are not particularly looking at anyone and you crossed their vision paths. They spend no more time looking at you than at any other person. Part of learning to minimize this feeling is being more self-confident and comfortable in your own skin. Partly, this comes with time and age, and partly, it comes from true self-confidence which comes from an inner belief in your own self-worth. The more we are able to challenge our faulty perceptions with our rational mind, the more we are able to dispel these uncomfortable feelings of having all eyes on us.

I feel that I can be easily hurt by the words of others. The feelings are so intense and out of proportion to what was probably intended. How do I stop overreacting?

The key to reducing the intensity is to practice catching ourselves early on when we initially feel the first signs of over arousal. By paying attention to how we feel when we become over aroused, we can have a plan in place to deescalate through removing ourselves from a situation and breathing to calm ourselves. The point is to reduce the emotions and engage our rational thinking capacities.

It also helps to be able to question our perceptions of what might have been said and exercise empathy for what the other person may have been feeling in the moment.

Some words are intended to be hurtful, no doubt, but misinterpreting what was said may cause us to overreact when, in fact, the overreaction is out of proportion. This speaks to the importance of having boundaries and enforcing those boundaries quite carefully!

Empowerment Points

- Perceptions in HS men may be faulty and unnecessarily causing suffering or limitations. Questioning our perceptions is crucial.
- The inner critic is strong in HS men and must be refuted and minimized through rational thinking and by relaxing the mind.
- Feedback can be constructive when given for the right reasons and can be very damaging when directed at a person's character or inherent worth.
- The Paul-Elder approach to critical thinking is an easy to use, readily communicable model we can employ to work through complex issues and gain greater context and understanding of a problem.
- One minute of courage may help us overcome social anxiety. Social anxiety is a learned behavior that can be unlearned. Do not let it limit your life.
- HS men may be psychologically androgynous and capable of inhabiting both ends of the spectrum while simultaneously appreciating what may appear to be dichotomous positions.

CHAPTER 6

Anger

"There's nothing either good or bad but thinking makes it so."
~William Shakespeare

It's been stated many times by the late Dr. Ted Zeff that anger is the only "approved emotion for HS men to express."[31] He meant socially approved when viewed through the lens of an extreme expression of masculinity, which exists in pockets throughout society. This book does not choose to express quite as strong a view as to presume that all men only express anger because they aren't allowed to express happiness, sadness, joy, tranquility, or any of a dozen other common emotions. Indeed, men, whether highly sensitive or not, may exhibit a range of emotions if we move beyond limiting views of masculinity. The problem of anger and subsequent violence is, however, an enormous problem in society and for men, but especially HS men.

Highly sensitive men learn early on, in many cases, that expressing what may be seen as "too much" emotion by parents, especially fathers, may be strongly disapproved of. Fathers who come from backgrounds where emotions are disapproved of may replicate the pattern of discouraging displays of emotion in their boys due to cultural pressure, though, many HS men report support from their mothers in expressing emotions. HS men feel this sense of disapproval quite deeply and the resulting aversion to displaying sensitivity may cause inner conflicts within the psyche for men as they seek to reconcile how they feel with how they think they should feel. HS men, owing to this special burden of feeling as if they must continually prove their manhood, may experience significant issues with emotion regulation.

Emotion Regulation

Sensory processing sensitivity, as a trait, works through strong, quick emotions that set off the chain of internal processing. With any kind of stimulation, one has to quickly decide if a certain stimulus is a threat, then move to a more general appraisal of priority. Pausing to think before acting is a hallmark of SPS and HS men, as well, prefer to think before acting. This longer processing time may run counter to the prevailing western notions of the quick-thinking and quick-acting man in charge and may lead many HS men to feel overwhelmed by both the need to consider the stimulation and the time pressure to act.

In such situations, HS men may feel frustrated, irritated, or simply angry at feeling an emotion they may not wish to and may not have time for. Anger, indeed, is quite evident in society as we encounter angry drivers, inconsiderate people in stores, malls, and workplaces, but there are likely just as many considerate people who will ignore a driver who cuts them off, dismiss the feeling of irritation at the fellow shopper who parks his cart diagonally in a store aisle, or find patience for a co-worker who is feeling angry that day. HS men, though they feel strong, quick emotions and may feel overwhelmed by several factors can learn to manage how they cope with their emotions.

There are several key points we should bear in mind regarding emotions:

- they are never permanent, what you are feeling now will pass.
- there truly is no reason to be ashamed of what we are feeling in each moment, since emotions are not aspects we get to choose.
- we can accept that we are feeling an emotion without judging it, thereby lessening its power over us.
- each person can learn to develop effective coping strategies.

We may not have all been taught how to cope with emotions as young boys, but we can and should learn those skills as HS men so that we can function effectively in our lives.

One of the most significant factors that complicates emotional regulation for HS men is the intensity with which we feel strong emotions. Couple that intensity with what we've learned as young boys as appropriate means of expression and HS men may often act out their emotions beyond conscious awareness. Nearly automatic responses complicate the process of how we feel, what we feel, and when we feel emotions.

The best strategy for emotion regulation is to gradually experiment with ways of mitigating how we experience an emotion and practicing labelling the emotion when we notice it. Moving an emotion, such as anger, into conscious awareness, demystifies it and allows us to examine why we may be feeling it at the moment. This conscious sense of awareness can then be coupled with the knowledge that it is only transient and will pass. Often, we can distract ourselves after we notice an emotion by taking a walk, being in nature, being near water, or working on an engaging project. The latter, for men, keys directly into our nature to build, fix, and construct reality.

Misophonia

There is another factor that may prove to be significant for some HS men in causing strong feelings of anger and rage. Misophonia is a phenomenon that about 15% of the total human population experiences in which certain types of trigger stimuli set off an immediate and disproportionate response in the individual. [64] That response is typically strong anger, rage, a need to escape the source of the stimulation, or what we might call fight, flee, or freeze.

Misophonia is not a disorder that has been recognized and does not appear in the diagnostic manual that psychotherapists use to confirm a diagnosis. We cannot even fairly say that Misophonia is a condition when the research does not support that conclusion. We can say that about 15% of the population experiences this phenomenon whereby trigger noises, visual cues, or other particular stimulation serve to produce a deeply uncomfortable feeling of immediate anger, rage, even panic in those who fall into the severe category.

How can you know whether you experience Misophonia and how it might be impacting your life as a HS man? There are three self-tests you can take that will help inform the way you experience Misophonia.

https://misophoniainstitute.org/misophonia-test-do-you-have-misophonia/

There is a brain basis for Misophonia that has been explored that seems to show how a region of the brain known as the anterior insula cortex (AIC), a key node of the brain's salience network, comes into play with Misophonia. The salience network in the brain is a large-scale network that detects and orients attention toward stimuli that are behaviorally relevant and meaningful for an individual. In the brains of those who experience Misophonia, there is greater salience assigned to specific types of triggers.[65]

This greater functional connectivity between the AIC and the ventromedial prefrontal cortex, posteromedial cortex, hippocampus, and the amygdala, coupled with greater myelination of nerve fibers (the fatty coating around nerve fibers that insulates them) leading to said regions serves to decrease reaction times to stimuli. The greater myelination of the nerve fibers increases the conduction of nerve impulses by a factor of 10 when compared to similarly sized unmyelinated nerve fibers. In fact, to achieve the same inter-hemispheric travel time for nerve impulses on unmyelinated axons would require a brain 100 times as large!

Misophonia is also associated with interoception, perception of internal bodily states, that may serve to influence the salience and experience of emotions associated with a given stimulus. This assignment of contextual associations to particular sounds or visual cues comes from the Default Mode Network (DMN), which is at work when we are at rest and not particularly considering the external world. The greater coupling of the AIC with the DMN seems to suggest that when a person experiencing Misophonia hears a trigger sound, he is unable to disengage the AIC from the DFN, thereby bringing the memories and other associations to bear on that trigger sound in an instant.

Trigger sounds are those generally made by the mouth, such as popping sounds, crunching, chewing, slurping, whispering, or other sounds. About 80% of trigger sounds are produced in that manner and the rest of the trigger sounds are produced in the external environment, including repetitive sounds, visual triggers, and others yet to be identified. The interesting aspect of those who experience Misophonic reactions to trigger sounds or visual cues is that they respond no differently than other people do to simple irritating sounds or neutral sounds. It's only the specific trigger sounds or visual cues that seem to set off the physical reflex that then becomes an emotional overreaction.

In HS men who experience Misophonia, it's not difficult to see how their already strong, quick, intense emotions are completely overloaded with the addition of Misophonia! Sensory processing sensitivity may moderate some of the effects of Misophonia in that the pause to think before acting that so characterizes SPS may serve to counterbalance, to some extent, the effects of Misophonia.

There are reasonably effective treatments for the experience of Misophonia for those in the severe category or the moderate category who need help with working out strategies for preempting the misophonic reflex. Typically, one would work with a therapist who specializes in the treatment of Misophonia to reframe the thoughts about trigger sounds using Cognitive Behavioral Therapy (CBT), which appear to be effective in about half the patients. Encouragingly, patients in the severe category seemed to be more likely to respond to treatment. This may be because they sincerely work hard to mitigate their Misophonia or that many of them may be HSPs, who, as we know, respond better to positive treatment interventions than do those without the trait due to Vantage Sensitivity.

Specialists who work with reducing Misophonic reactions focus on interrupting the physical reflex that sets off the emotional overreaction. Using a technique called Progressive Muscle Relaxation, therapists teach clients to notice the muscle that clenches upon hearing a trigger sound. For many the stomach muscles clench, for others, it may be the shoulders that tighten, or another muscle or muscles. By focusing on breathing and intentionally relaxing the triggered muscle, one can very effectively halt the progression of Misophonia.[66] This does require a good deal of work but can greatly reduce Misophonic overreactions, when combined with CBT. As a moderate category Misophonic, I can attest to the extreme nature of the overreactions and how deeply they can impact one's life.

Quick story: my dad was likely a Misophonic who felt triggered by sounds made by the mouth, certain visual cues, and others that would activate him to anger and lashing out verbally at others. He was, of course, not aware of his Misophonia because few people today are even aware that it exists. Much of the quick emotions, anger, irritability, and the way he would avoid social occasions limited his life and his potential, though he was quite an intelligent man. I have realized over time, since he passed away when I was 15, that he was very likely Misophonic and a HS man, but was never aware of it, nor would he have ever accepted it or adapted his life. We, however, are aware of Misophonia and SPS and living in a time when great information is readily available, and differences are far more acceptable in men.

The Angry Dad

Did you have an angry dad? Were you leery of saying the wrong thing or otherwise failing to meet his high standards? Did your dad seem easily irritated and annoyed? You're not alone, as many HS men seem to report the "angry dad scenario" and many of us spend a good portion of our lives trying to reconcile the sources of that anger. Often, it is because our dads were likely HS men themselves, only they didn't have a clue that they were sensitive and likely would have never been okay with this concept.

I'm speaking to you now from the heart as a 53 year old man who grew up with an often angry dad who was stressed, usually because he lacked coping strategies, worked odd shifts at work, and liked to fight, binge drink at times, and he could be quite cruel with words and actions. There was domestic abuse at times in my home growing up, there was a real sense of fear about how my dad would be on any given day. He seemed to be most happy when he was at work but returned to a sketchy baseline of behavior and attitude otherwise. Oddly, his father was fairly even-tempered and a truly kind man (my grandfather).

Being the son of an angry parent, especially a father, can be quite difficult and may serve to stunt one's normal growth and development, as boys may gain a fear of all men or suffer from low self-esteem, lack of self-confidence, and feeling as if they have no personal power. We know from Vantage Sensitivity that we HSPs do less well than average when in unsupportive environments. We also know the role of Adverse Childhood Experiences (ACEs) in limiting our lives when we suffer from a chaotic, fearful, abusive, or neglectful early beginning.

Healing from having an angry dad is beyond the scope of this book, but we must acknowledge the role our angry dads may have unwittingly played as a result of their not having addressed their emotional and behavioral issues. Many HS men that I have interviewed over the years have communicated the same angry dad scenario where they felt their core being was not acceptable to their dads. The damage from not feeling accepted can be immense and lead to us becoming angry dads ourselves packing around unsettled emotional baggage.

Self-Compassion, Self-Parenting, Self-Friending

"...tomorrow and plans for tomorrow can have no significance at all unless you are in full contact with the reality of the present, since it is in the present and only in the present that you live" ~Alan Watts

We HS men may be very hard on ourselves emotionally as we process messages of shame, differentness, and non-acceptance. We also tend to suffer more in silence than we should. Too many of us have inadequate support systems to rely on for simple human connection. Research tells us that even having one close friend to confide in leads to better health outcomes as we age. [67] Along with having at least one close ongoing friendship, we HS men can benefit greatly from learning to be self-compassionate.

Self-compassion enfolds self-parenting and self-friending in an empathetic and loving way that may work especially well for introverted HS men. How do we get to self-compassion? One way is to turn that high empathy we HSPs are well-known for around and focus it on ourselves. It is all the more appropriate that we develop the capacity to feel empathy for what we experience in life and that empathy should lead us to compassion. Practicing self-compassion, self-parenting, and self-friending enables us to feel less lonely, to self-soothe more effectively, and to develop a sense of self-love through identifying with ourselves objectively, as a friend might.

What about self-parenting? What does that look like?

Critical Self-Parenting: this style of self-parenting involves always looking at the pessimistic and negative aspects and never recognizing or acknowledging that we are all imperfect human beings. Critical self-parenting is tearing yourself down bit by bit instead of building yourself up with love, patience, and compassion.

Neglectful Self-Parenting: in this style, we never deal with problems and put them off as if they will disappear if we just don't think about them. By failing to provide motivation to enact meaningful change, we lock ourselves into a spiral of anxiety and depression that is unable to be lifted.

Loving Self-Parenting: approaching self-parenting as an exercise in love and kindness is a far better approach than either critical or neglectful. When our self-talk is positive, kind, loving, and motivates us to take self-affirmative and constructive actions, we embrace our own power and become the loving parents many of us did not have in childhood.

Once we develop and grow the capacity to be a loving self-parent, we become more aware of our inner processes and how to support and encourage our best intentions throughout life. Through a continual process of self-reflection – always with patience and kindness – we may come to experience what our true essence is, at its core. This active, engaged process is aimed at helping us to coordinate our mental life in positive and generative ways that allow us to, in effect, become our own teachers and psychotherapists.

Autopsychotherapy or Self-Analysis

"Through the constant creation of himself, through the development of the inner psychic milieu and development of discriminating power with respect to both the inner and outer milieus – an individual goes through ever higher levels of 'neuroses' and at the same time through ever higher levels of universal development of his personality" ~Kazimierz Dabrowski

Autopsychotherapy, or self-analysis if you prefer, may seem like an odd concept but HS men may be naturally inclined towards self-examination and reflection as a matter of our deep processing of experience and need for self-growth. Carrying this further, we can learn to guide ourselves during periods of distress and crisis in ways that are uniquely suited to our individual dispositions. No one knows you better than yourself and no one will be able to discern how well an approach to a situation worked as well as you.

Learning to be your own therapist and trying on custom-tailor strategies and coping skills that will work for you in trying times will empower you to not only address what you need to do in an immediate way but also provide for your long-term growth and development as a whole person capable of self-soothing and growth through the inevitable crisis' we all encounter throughout life.

Autopsychotherapy is not weird or strange, it's simply being aware of your thoughts, patterns of behaviors, and inclinations when you are in a crisis and working out ways to address issues that are troubling you. The psychoanalyst Karen Horney believed that every person has a drive toward self-realization, much as an acorn becomes an oak tree over time. It is our lack of a supportive and nurturing environment that stunts our growth or limits our ability to self-realize, the same for the acorn in poor soil, it does not grow or mature as well as it might. Horney stated, "the human individual, given a chance, tends to develop...the unique alive forces of his real self, the clarity and depth of his own feelings, thoughts, wishes, interests; the ability to tap his own resources, the strength of his will power... he will grow, substantially undiverted, toward self-realization."[68] It is when we experience unsupportive environments in early life that we develop anxieties and neuroses, or anger, and only later that we develop attempts to feel safe in what we perceive to be an unsafe world.

These holdovers from childhood damage represent inner work we can do that Horney describes as providing an "extra gain in having conquered inner territory entirely through one's own initiative, courage, and perseverance."[68]

Being your own therapist will help you become more self-reliant emotionally and will better equip you to relate to others as they have their own issues. There are instances, of course, where one should seek professional help, such as having suicidal thoughts, depressions that refuse to lift, and other issues where an objective viewpoint would be of value. Learning to be more self-aware of our anger as HS men and making choices to replace that emotion with patience, tolerance, or benevolence may be a monumental task for some, but the main factor that will determine success in self-analysis is our own desire for self-realization.

Highly sensitive men, by nature, are reflective and will seek self-improvement just as the acorn seeks to become an oak tree. Ridding ourselves of anger may take some years and a great deal of work to heal our inner psyche. Anger, and the problems it brings in relationships, career, and overall life satisfaction deserves our attention if we aim to move towards becoming whole persons. Carl Jung said that we spend our lives in search of wholeness, though the bigger intent is self-perfection.[69] The same individuation impulse of Jung impels us to seek out and bring to light the dark elements of our "shadow selves" in pursuit of integration.

Many HS men have, unfortunately, had the experience of feeling invalidated as men early on. Some were told they were "too sensitive," or had a "bad temper," but many were likely reacting to disapproval from parents and others seeking to mold and shape them into narrow definitions of manhood as seen by culture. There is a real anger that gets repressed as we grow and come of age, a feeling of anger about being "different" or less than others.

That anger gets shoved all too often into our "shadow sides" and asserts itself throughout life as a hidden ghost, always testifying to how we are living as less than whole persons. That hidden anger can manifest itself in destructive ways the more we refuse to address it. It's in our quiet times, away from others in public, that our "shadow sides" often compel us to self-destructive behaviors seemingly out of conscious awareness.

To effectively deal with our shadow sides, we have to admit an awareness that they exist and then become aware of our moods, fantasies, and tendencies. Often, we think of doing things that show us that our sense of aggression was interfered with early on and never allowed to find productive channeling. It is through a process of self-negotiation that we can learn to connect anger with aggression in healthy ways like being more assertive, connecting with our physical bodies through a sport, for example, or exploring our inner worlds with purpose and determination.

Questions and answers

Are all HS men angry?

Not at all, anger is a cultural issue, particularly in the US where men are taught to suppress emotions and always appear strong and dominant. Anger may be rooted in many underlying causes but the primary one we are concerned with for HS men has to do with anger that is just under the surface and permeates one's character as a result of abuse, neglect, chaos in the home, or other trauma. Many HS men come from completely loving and supportive environments and may be indistinguishable from other men except for the emotional sensitivity. The long-term limiting effects are significant for those who have accumulated resentments, repressed emotions or feelings, or who have lived as less than their whole being.

What else can cause me to feel so angry?

Anger can come from many sources such as driving in traffic, being in situations where we feel we have no control, or, as in the case of those who experience Misophonia, anger can be quick and immediate due to trigger sounds. We can also feel angry due to overthinking about things in our lives or at our workplace. Many things can trigger anger or irritation when one has strong, quick emotions that lead to deep processing of stimuli. Learning to deescalate is the key so rational thinking can come back into play.

What is especially bad about anger for HS men?

It's the intensity which we feel with anger that is truly the damaging factor. Research tells us that HSPs fare worse in negative environments and there isn't a much worse environment than any angry one. Anger in ourselves or in other people will quickly overstimulate us and take us out of our natural balance. We need to work on establishing and enforcing our boundaries to keep anger at bay and prevent us from escalating beyond a point where it becomes overstimulating and all encompassing.

<u>**Empowerment Points**</u>

- HS men often feel a sense of anger just under the surface that may stem from childhood non-acceptance or directed at the self as a result of faulty perceptions.

- An angry feeling is just a passing moment; let it pass.
- Misophonia may be a confounding factor for HS men in producing anger. Misophonia can be mitigated through various therapeutic interventions.
- Becoming self-compassionate can help us develop self-empathy and a greater capacity for self-love.
- HS men are the acorns desperately trying to be the oak trees.

CHAPTER 7

The Creative Life and Life as Creative

"There is a vitality, a life force, an energy, a quickening that is translated through you into action, and because there is only one of you in all time, this expression is unique. And if you block it, it will never exist through any other medium and will be lost." ~Martha Graham

In any discussion of HS men, we must explore the creative life and creativity directed at creating our lives. The reason for this is the many descriptions of sensitivity as creative by definition, meaning to be aware of subtleties, to process experience, feelings, and thoughts deeply, to be curious and open, and to feel the energies of others, all seem to add up to what we commonly imply when we use the word "creativity."

This does not mean that all HS men are actively engaged in creative projects or careers, but that they do carry the strong possibility of being more open to new stimuli, ideas, and possibilities than others. HS men are in all careers, even fields where one would not necessarily expect them to be, such as the military, where it is entirely possible to work in a skill that simultaneously and ironically, may work well for the HS man. Speaking from experience as a veteran of the U.S. Army, I can attest to the fact that HS men may turn up anywhere! It is impossible to stereotype HS men and it is unfair to do so because relegating them to a narrow container denies the complexity and flexibility of sensory processing sensitivity and the plasticity of the human being. How do HS men embody creativity in different ways?

The Creative Life

Before we begin to discuss the creative life, let's first carefully define what we mean by "creative" and dispel deeply ingrained cultural beliefs about the term. Creativity has long been associated only with the realm of the artist, who has been cast as the outsider, the loner, the suffering madman.[70] Creativity has also been devalued in society despite much talk about a desire for creative solution and innovation. Creativity and the exploratory, formative process that it entails takes time, energy, and may be ambiguous for a time as the process unfolds.

Let's talk about an often overlooked and unacknowledged relationship. I'm talking about the give and take that exists between creative thinking and critical thinking. Just as the painter makes marks on a canvas and steps back to assess what he has done, the process of creating has embedded within it an equally important evaluative process. Our ability to discern, to compare and rank, is what we mean by critical thinking. Forget the idea that critical means to demean, critical in critical thinking means to discern. Critical thinking, then, is to discern using universal standards of thinking that allow us to think efficiently, accurately, and fairly, while focused on a complex problem.[63]

To think creatively is to be the wide part of a funnel where new ideas can flow in and be entertained for a while in exploration before being assessed and ranked. The funnel, then, narrows at one end as we engage critical thinking and begin evaluating the ideas that we have allowed in. The two processes work hand in hand and are inseparable, synergistic, and interdependent.[71] We simply cannot have creative thinking without a commiserate criticality that can assess and evaluate what we have generated and produced. Likewise, we cannot have meaningful critical thinking without ideas, options, and alternatives to assess. See how they work together? That's what we mean by critical creative thinking.

Using this broader perspective of what it means to be critical creative thinkers, we can now begin to see that there are a million ways to apply this innately human process of inventing new ideas, concepts, and ways of doing things. Not all HS men will consider themselves to be critical creative thinkers, as many will likely share the same misunderstandings about creativity, as are so common in society. However, it does seem that when we look at the qualities HS men embody through SPS that the propensity is there to be more open, to feel the experiences of other living things, to notice nuances and subtleties others miss entirely, and to think about things in a way that combines deep intuition with a sense of curiosity about what might be possible.

How might critical creative thinking play out in your life and how might you cultivate it intentionally? For one, both require practice to become effective; otherwise, they both exist at a relatively modest level in most people. One can learn to think creatively when one understands what that means more clearly. Divergent thinking is often cited as being indicative of the creative thinking process and entails what is fundamentally an emergent, exploratory process of generating and following ideas. In divergent thinking judgements are deferred to allow time for the brainstorming process to unfold without prematurely rushing to assessment. Creative thinking may also be thought of as horizontal thinking that seeks to explore and gather ideas, concepts, and possibilities before engaging in evaluating and ranking.

Many innately creative people, including HS men, relate to creative thinking well but not necessarily to critical thinking. Critical thinking is ambiguous in society and, while most people will acknowledge that it is important to learn, few are prepared to practice critical thinking in the real world. To become a more rational thinker is a process that, like creative thinking, becomes easier with greater understanding and practice over a lifetime.

For years, I have taught critical thinking to students in the master's program that I oversee at Baker University using the Paul-Elder approach. Drs. Richard Paul and Linda Elder advocate for a critical thinking practice that is easily communicable and reasonable to understand and implement because it is immediately applicable to real life. More on the Paul-Elder approach to critical thinking may be found in the book, Critical Thinking: Tools for Taking Charge of Your Professional and Personal Life, and at criticalthinking.org.

The Experience of Flow

Along with the interplay between creative and critical thinking, HS men will especially benefit from flow experiences. Positive psychologist, Mihaly Csikszentmihalyi, originated the flow concept as a psychological construct but humans have always experienced flow states because it is in our nature to create and to focus intently on a challenging task. [72] Csikszentmihalyi further posited that it has always been in the interest of survival of the species that a small group of its members are hardwired for novelty, exploration, and discovery.

Csikszentmihalyi defines flow as comprising nine key aspects:

1. There are clear goals every step of the way.
2. There is immediate feedback to one's actions.
3. There is balance between challenges and skills.
4. Action and awareness are merged.
5. Distractions are excluded from consciousness.
6. There is no worry of failure.
7. Self-consciousness disappears.
8. The sense of time becomes distorted.
9. The activity becomes autotelic.

If this sounds too complex, consider that flow states can happen in any instance where the task is challenging, there is immediate feedback, and one becomes absorbed in the task at hand for a time. Indeed, Csikszentmihalyi, believes that experiencing flow states regularly is essential for happiness and well-being.

Most creative HS men are familiar with the flow state, either explicitly or intuitively, and appreciate the feeling of challenge versus skills. Even more encouragingly, flow states for HS men allow for a time free of anxiety and boredom. The flow state is best thought of as a stream with anxiety on one side and boredom on the other. Anxiety results when the task at hand is more than we are capable of and boredom results from either a lack of engagement or a less than challenging task where skills are greater than the task.

Life as Creative

"On a high level of development creative instinct becomes an instinct of self-perfection which besides the media of artistic expression begins to stress more and more strongly the concern for inner perfection"
~Kazimierz Dabrowski

Beyond life as a creative individual, the HS man may be gifted or high in developmental potential. This innate potential, according to the theory of positive disintegration, constitutes a lifelong process of growth and development interspersed by crises and disintegrations, only to reintegrate at higher levels of development. According to psychologist Kazimierz Dabrowski, originator of the theory, the creative instinct has no greater application than the realization of inner potential.[40]

Not all people will be high in developmental potential, but for those who are, the path becomes less guided and influenced by social forces and the ego and leans more towards altruism and self-chosen life paths. Many of the HS men I have spoken with have expressed to me a similar path that has wound through their lives wherein they left behind old ideas and notions that only served to reinforce early shame or hurt and instead embraced self-development. When viewed in this light, life becomes much richer and more rewarding in truly knowing who we are and what we can become over a lifetime.

The key aspect that distinguishes how creativity is used to create a life is the degree to which one has the drive to shape life rather than to be shaped by it. At the same time, we begin to leave off the dictates of society and begin to increase our self-awareness we also, perhaps consciously or not, direct our creative energies at exploring and generating options that will move us more toward what we wish to be and less toward what we feel we ought to be, as defined by society. What steps can you take to become more of who you feel yourself to be at your core? What is holding you back from stepping into your power?

There are several skills we can cultivate and practice as we move towards greater self-awareness and self-development:

1. Tame the monkey mind. We are primates with a tendency to catastrophize the next crisis or disaster and can easily spend too much time with overflowing and repetitive thoughts that lead us nowhere.
2. Allow your wholeness. So many HS men are shaped and formed by societal pressures to make them less than whole in the name of conformity. Our task is to allow the full range of our inherent potentiality to live freely, then to be open to what that brings.
3. Be your own internal power source. Live life for its own sake and not to find validation or praise from others. Seek meaning. This is your unique life with only one chance to come into your wholeness as a being on this planet.
4. Follow and nurture curiosity. Curiosity is the fundamental proposition of the universe. What can happen in your life if you are open to following a path that is different than any you have ever travelled?
5. Commune with likeminded others. The majority of people will be guided by society, seek out those who

are strong enough to forge their own unique paths and learn from them!

6. Know that it is all play. Life is not as terribly serious as we imagine it to be. Reclaim your open, playful approach to life knowing that we are meant to dance while the music plays.

Life itself, as a creative act, is forever unfolding, blossoming, and renewing itself. We HS men are uniquely positioned and equipped with a trait that predisposes us to the inner life of thought, self-directed actions, and self-betterment, if we are in supportive environments. Dabrowski taught that people with high developmental potential would develop whether in good or bad environments but would grow much better in a good environment.[41] If your life unfolds in some corner of the Earth where you feel out of touch with everyone else and alone in pushing yourself to grow beyond the mold that others around you seem so eager to fit, it is likely that you will continue to develop in place, regardless.

I can attest to the idea of "developing in place" as a HSS/HS man growing up in small town Missouri where few were interested in deeper topics or anything beyond sociocentric and egocentric conformity. How did I become the man I am today? Through long suffering and a belief that I could and should do more for my self-realization. Nothing will demonstrate to you just how very different you are than being in the daily company of people who you do not share a worldview with. The world will tell you to "just conform like everyone else," but your head and heart will compel you to seek application for your deep mind, your innate creativity, and your broad range.

It's been said that most HSPs simply do not know themselves well enough until mid-life to truly grow into full blossom. Too often, we get lost in the wilderness of daily life and sublimate our deeper needs. I invite you to think of life itself as a fundamentally creative process that is ever-unfolding, just like the processes of our universe itself. What and who can you become if you push through fear? How can you change your world, and potentially the world of others, if you see life with new eyes? What greater meaning can you bring to life if you think of life as a creative process? Just imagine...

Questions and answers

How can I relate to creativity if I am not an artist?

By reframing how we view creativity. Creative thinking is part and parcel of critical thinking because we need to both generate ideas (creative thinking) and evaluate and assess them (critical thinking). We need both to be working in synergy to be at our full potential. Creativity is for everyone at any time. Artists and creatives have no special propensity for creativity other than being more open and willing to tolerate greater ambiguity in the exploration process. Anyone can learn to think more creatively and critically.

I've always felt like I am living beneath my abilities and never really blossoming, how can I live life as a creative process?

As a HS man you likely have very worthy developmental potential but may have struggled with fitting in in a culture that does not seem to fit you. Your task is to align your life with your needs and prioritize your growth and development beyond fulfilling societal expectations.

Thinking of life as a creative act is simply seeing that we are all part of an uncertain and uncontrollable process that is an illusion our egos seek to control and dominate. Working to lessen our egos will open us up to opportunities in life that will push our growth and development.

Empowerment Points

- HS men may direct their creativity as creative production or at producing an original life.
- Critical creative thinking is the process of both generating and assessing our ideas. We need both to be in balance and present in our thinking.
- The flow state engages us in a way no other experience may hope to. We should be in flow states often.
- Life may be viewed as an inherently creative process, ever unfolding and rich with possibilities.
- Step into your power with confidence and ease.

CHAPTER 8

Self-Care and Highly Sensitive Men

"You're in pretty good shape for the shape you're in!" ~Dr. Seuss

Self-care for all HSPs is a crucial aspect of maintaining a sustainable way of life, given that we expend a great deal more energy absorbing and processing stimulation than in less sensitive people. HS men face the double burden of the usual self-care we HSPs need so desperately: adequate sleep, reducing stress, right diet, effective boundaries, and a life that truly fits us, but also must manage the additional complication of being more complex psychologically and emotionally than is approved of in the culture. Many HS men are invalidated early on in a dozen ways by parents and others who often act blindly out of conformity and fear that a HS boy may not fit in or be accepted.

They are right, of course, in that many HS boys find themselves told to not be themselves or to simply "toughen up!" Our natural tendency for pausing to think before we act bothers faster thinking types who often act rashly and suffer consequences but nonetheless feel that fast thinking is the only acceptable way. In this chapter, we will look at the crucial components that all HS men need to address to allow for moving beyond simply living with sensory processing sensitivity, itself a neutral personality trait that is neither positive nor negative.

Right Diet

There is a great deal of disagreement about which diet we should follow. Diet fads are all over the news in 2020 from paleo, vegan, vegetarian, Ketogenic, and Atkins to MediKeto and Mediterranean. How we eat is also deeply personal and many people cling to eating habits out of identification with a culture or familiarity with associations through food. With the theme of right diet as our guiding concern, let's examine a few salient points for your consideration.

You Are What You Eat

How many times have we all heard the familiar refrain, yet seem to be in denial about how what we choose to consume becomes what we are? Many people today seem to ignore cause and effect and choose foods that raise blood pressure, contribute to heart disease, and promote inflammation throughout the body. Inflammation, as we now know, is implicated in many, if not most, of the deleterious diseases afflicting humankind. The kicker? It's not that difficult to reduce inflammation and avoid foods that contribute to poor long-term health. Just as a runner must think in terms of the 26-mile race, we must also think in terms of how what we eat today becomes what we are tomorrow.

The standard American diet, for example, is promoted as healthful but is upside down in the worst way. Most of the food pyramid is based on faulty science and heavily lobbied for by the food industry, which has never had your or my best interests at heart. The standard American diet is typically very high in carbohydrate intake, high in refined sugar consumption, loaded with hidden ingredients that act like sugar in the body, low in healthy fats, devoid of real nutrition, and caters to an addictive mentality where food is seen as the opium of the diner.

Changing how we relate to food is our first task as we reframe the purpose of eating: to promote health and healing in the body. Just as we would not put diesel fuel in a gasoline engine, why would we choose to put poor-quality fuels into the vehicle that carries us through life and that depends on our choices for its fuel? Our bodies are amazing ecosystems of interdependent and synergistic individual systems that work together to allow consciousness, movement, and a well-functioning system. We eat to provide optimum fuel for our bodies for best performance.

We know that high carbohydrate intake is how we can turn people into diabetics.[73] That process has been known for decades, though little promoted, with more attention turned to fat and cholesterol and its demeaning effects on health, though there is no good science to back up the health industry's claims and subsequent advice to doctors. Doctors, for their part, unfortunately, receive little training in nutrition and many do not remain current on the latest research. This means we are on our own to decide what we should be eating for optimum health and longevity and that we will have to learn how to find and vet information on our own.

With a skeptical and discerning eye, we read articles, books, and published peer reviewed studies to break through the hype, fads, and mistruths. As HS men, we find ourselves more energetically taxed than those without the trait, meaning high empathy and the absorption of energies, especially negative energies, is depleting to say the least. The modern workplace and modern life in general is rushed, stressed, and the burden is placed squarely on the shoulders of the individual. If you don't have enough income, society says that it's your fault, regardless of systemic issues that should be addressed. That's just the reality of life today and it is depleting for many HS men as they struggle to find ways to provide for their family's needs and their own sense of self-actualization.

How Should We Eat?

Each person must choose which foods to consume and which to avoid, while acknowledging there are tradeoffs in each case. Should you choose to consume foods cooked in highly refined oils, you suffer with inflammation. If you choose to consume foods that our bodies are not adapted to process in such steady quantities, like fruit, we risk burning out our pancreas and becoming a type 2 diabetic. I will take no strict position on diet but will advise that there are several very good non-fad diets, or ways of eating, that will promote health and well-functioning. You will have to decide how deeply you are invested in health and how willing you are to make changes, if need be.

One way you do not need to take anyone's word for it is to check your own blood sugars at 30 minutes, 60 minutes, and 90 minutes after consuming any food or meal. Anyone may buy an inexpensive glucometer and test strips at many stores or online. The 60-minute point is generally where you will see the peak rise in blood sugar and it should decline from there, if you have a normally functioning pancreas. For example, you might choose to consume white bread and see how it affects you. Perhaps your body processes it better than others or perhaps not, but you'll never know unless you actually check your blood. There is also a test your doctor can do for you called an A1C that will check your blood sugar over time but that will not tell you how an individual food acts in your body.

If you're already type 2 diabetic, then you are familiar with this advice, but, if not, the only way to judge which foods may be "safe" to consume is through the dreaded finger sticks. You might also wish to try the Continuous Glucose Monitor (CGM), available by prescription from your doctor. The CGM is a sensor that is attached to your arm and remains in place for two weeks. It has a small needle that pokes under the skin and reads your blood sugar every five minutes and relays that information through an app on your phone. As time progresses, we are likely to see far more technology like the CGM and other monitoring and sensing devices that may be used to gather real-time data from our bodily systems.

We HS men need to be especially careful with diet because our bodies are already stressed as a matter of processing all stimulation more deeply than less sensitive people. Fueling our bodies in ways that are appropriate for our own individual body chemistries and genome appears to be the future of nutrition and only makes sense when we consider that no two people's gut biome are the same and will tolerate foods differently.

Reducing stress

"Resistance creates suffering. Stress happens when your mind resists what is. The only problem in your life is your mind's resistance to life as it unfolds" ~Dan Millman

HS men, like all HSPs, may feel more stressed during daily life as they navigate a ceaselessly moving and demanding world where little value is placed on the inner life of reflection, contemplation, or solitude. It is ironic that many HS men may rise to positions of success in the world yet be unprepared for the rigors that accompany promotions and enormous responsibilities. Burnout is common as many HS men push themselves to be less of who they truly are and more of what the world demands. HSPs, based on several studies, seem to place less emphasis on the influence of culture, yet we are all immersed in its insidious grasp and breaking free from narrowly defined roles will lessen stress almost automatically.

When we subscribe to the idea that we HS men should conform to culture's arbitrarily decided values, norms, and beliefs, we do ourselves a disservice. We HS men, by definition, are wired a bit differently and intended by evolution to serve a slightly different function within social groups. This doesn't mean it has ever been easy for HS men to contribute to their social groups, but the value of deep thinking and creativity coupled with rationality, empathy, and openness should be obvious in its worth.

Part of the resistance we feel may be that HS men may be high in developmental potential (some may indeed be gifted individuals) and find themselves in relatively unchallenging work.[40] Boredom is a significant problem for many HSPs as their capacities may not align with their position. This may be especially true for the HS man who is also high in sensation seeking because his need to remain within his optimal range of stimulation may feel quite pressing. For HS men, they may feel less of a need for novelty and new experiences but still bore when faced with repetition or unchallenging work or situations.

Feeling stressed as a result of mismatch in skills and abilities means we are not in a flow state regularly enough.

You've heard about the flow state in other places in this book and may recall that flow is a state where one is engaged in a challenging task that provides immediate feedback, where skills are matched to the task, and where there is unusual motivation to stay with the task because it becomes worth doing for its own sake. How does flow reduce stress? When in the flow state all anxieties and worries seem to fall away as we engage fully with the task at hand. We are present, and present in the moment.

My personal flow story

In the spring of 2019, I decided to build a mini camper. I have previous building experience and know how to use power tools, fastening systems, and have never been a stranger to hard physical work. Over the next two months, I hauled in a new 5 x 10 flatbed trailer to construct the camper on and all the materials. Working inside my garage, I spent many long hours sawing, drilling and driving screws to construct the floor, walls, and roof. Each project of the mini camper was new to me as I had never built one before. Indulging my love of building things and creating, I fell into a flow state so easily each day and would spend a few hours accomplishing the task I set out for that day.

I cannot adequately express to you how much I enjoyed the entire process, splinters, cuts, bruises, and scrapes! At each point, there was research to be conducted, how to insulate the floor, what to use for the inside and outside walls, and which roofing material do I select?

Choices had to be made each step of the way and lots of innovation had to be implemented where I had to work out how to solve a problem, they always cropped up. I loved it! HS men, if you have never been in a flow state, you are truly missing real happiness! I also truly enjoyed the feeling of solid, rugged manliness in handling power tools, drilling and driving screws, and pushing my physicality to accomplish what should have taken two people in many instances.

You do not need to build a mini-camper or anything at all to de-stress or enter a flow state. You could take up walking, running, biking, hiking, skiing, snowboarding, archery, or any activity that gets you moving consistently and that you enjoy. Our bodies are made for movement, made to work with our hands, arms, legs, eyes, and brain. We are not meant for sitting and sedentary activities. We also are not made for high stress, which can quickly lead to emotion-driven thinking and overstimulation. Mastering our own minds and how we react to stimulation, events, and circumstances takes practice, mentoring, and patience, but in time, many HS men can become quite good at learning to calm themselves and minimize their stress levels throughout the day.

The value of touch

The very first sense that we have as newborns is touch. We can sense physical contact and warmth before seeing or hearing and for good reason as we are prosocial beings who need caring others to help sustain and nurture us. Physical touch is essential for physical and psychological health and well-being. When we hug, for example, our bodies release a hormone called Oxytocin that reduces our stress. Our blood pressure also lowers when we hug or are hugged. Touch also helps to reduce feelings of loneliness, one of the key factors in a person's longevity.

The power of human touch has long been suspected to provide healing abilities to partners and spouses but now research conducted by Pavel Goldstein at CU Boulder seems to demonstrate that we are able to sync up our physiology through touch.[74] Goldstein's team found that women who were touched by their husbands had their pain levels reduced and their heart and respiration rates synced up again versus when husbands did not touch and only observed when the women were subjected to mild heat pain.

Dr. Goldstein's previous studies showed that a woman feels less pain the more empathetic a man is towards her. For HS men, the role of touch is a powerful one and one that most of us are acutely aware of. We may crave being touched and wither without it. HS women, as well, need to be touched by their partners. Whether your partner or spouse is highly sensitive doesn't matter with regards to touch as all humans may benefit from simple touching. Now, there are HSPs and HS men who seemingly have aversions to being touched, which may indicate that they feel overwhelmed by the stimulation. If your partner has such an aversion, it may be advisable to work to find ways of touching that do not overstimulate, perhaps a lighter touch or a shorter duration would work.

Some people are not hand holders and will never feel comfortable doing so, but they may be entirely comfortable with a hug or a caress. Each person has to find the ways that feel most comfortable and natural to provide touch to others. HS men may have to work at this to feel comfortable in giving simple human touch to others because they may have never received it themselves. It takes a caring and patient partner who understands that emotional vulnerability takes time and trust to develop to be effective in encouraging touch. HS men may be natural responders to healing touch as they see the immediate effects on their partners and wish to sustain that positive and supportive environment.

We also know that HS men will likely be quicker to respond to touch simply because HSPs in general tend to respond more quickly in therapeutic approaches. What if there isn't a partner or spouse around to touch? What does a single man do? One can receive many of the same benefits of touch by having a pet to touch. As we know, pets generally love all the touch we can give them! If you really want to practice your sense of touch, try it out on a cat. Cats are exquisitely sensitive creatures who respond to even slight movements. Note how the pressure of your touch has an effect on the cat's somatic reactions. Also note how certain areas are favored by the cat as preferred touch points such as the cheeks and behind the ears. I am privileged enough to share my life with a female Siamese cat who is no doubt highly sensitive, and it is fascinating to observe how she responds to very light touch.

When I was a divorced, single man in my late 30s and dating, one of the things that I seemed to do that other men did not do, according to the women I knew, was touch. This gets into intimate touch, but I often found that caressing a woman's back with a light touch was practically unknown to them! Few, if any, men had ever taken the time or put forth the effort to get to know their bodies in that way. This form of touch was unexpected from a man and quite different from what they had experienced in the past. Not only is touch good for your partner, but it's also so good for you as well!

Exercise

"Exercise is a celebration of what your body can do. Not a punishment for what you ate" ~Anonymous

Our bodies are designed to move yet we sit far too much, get our heartrates up far too little, and miss the benefits that accompany a moderate exercise program. HS men will benefit from regular exercise that gets the heart rate up to a moderate level and sustains it for some time. You don't need to run marathons, but you do need to move, whether that means walking, hiking, bicycling, swimming, dancing, or other forms of movement, yes, including sexual activity.[75]

There's a myth that deserves to be broken here: that HS men do not prefer competitive sports or playing on teams. It might be fine to say that some HS men would not prefer to play in ultra-competitive circumstances but make no mistake, no two HS men are alike. Some of us may well enjoy playing in an adult softball league, soccer, football, bowling team or sport of your choice. Many of us are also likely to prefer participation in individual sports like running, archery, cycling, surfing or other events where the real goal is to do one's best each time around. All methods of participating are equally valid and very likely apply to the broad cross section of HS men.

The best exercise you can do is the one you will stay with and practice regularly. It does little good to start a new exercise, only to stop a few weeks or months later when the novelty has worn off. Personally, I choose walking at a brisk pace as my preferred exercise and I do it year-round, barring exceptionally bad weather because I walk outside on a trail that is next to a flowing river. I am able to simultaneously be immersed in nature and take my daily walk!

It is advisable to take stock of your physical health if you have not exercised in a while. You do not want to overdo it with a strenuous exercise your body is not used to and find yourself injured or worsening an existing health condition. It is preferable that you get a yearly physical exam at a doctor and work out a reasonable exercise program based on your health limitations and abilities. Always start off slow and build your endurance over time. My brisk walk evolved over time as a result of slowly pushing my abilities until my body responded by enhancing my endurance.

The role of exercise becomes particularly important as we age. If you are young, now is a great time to build lifetime exercise habits. If you are midlife, it's still a great time to build new habits, even if you are a senior, exercise should be one sustained aspect of your overall self-care practice. Make time for it every day and know that by engaging in physical exercise, you are doing your body and mind a world of good!

Sleep

"Sleep is the golden chain that ties health and our bodies together"
~Thomas Dekker

It's been said that quality sleep is the cornerstone of good mental health. HS men need to ensure they get adequate sleep each night. HSPs, in general, may need more sleep than less sensitive people so there is no need to feel bad about sleeping more than others. Your body is simply hardwired differently and functions in a slightly different way and it requires quality sleep to recover from each day's stimulation.

Here is where I implore you to consider diet again because your diet may be contributing to your lack of ability to sleep or to experience low quality sleep where you either have trouble falling or staying asleep. There is a simple way that you can test how diet may be affecting your sleep: simply reduce one or more categories of food and see what happens to your sleep quality. I recommend reducing your sugar intake first then follow with reducing your carbohydrate consumption and see what happens. In my case, once I reduced my carbohydrate intake, eliminated sugars, and avoided highly processed oils, my sleep quality improved overnight! I went from fidgety sleep where I often awoke to deep sleep where I only awoke after many hours! If the solution to your sleep problem was simply to reduce your consumption of certain foods, and avoid having to take chemicals to sleep, why wouldn't you try? I'll never go back; I love my deep sleep!

Setting and Maintaining Effective Boundaries

"Your personal boundaries protect the inner core of your identity and your right to choices" ~Gerard Manley Hopkins

Highly sensitive men tend to be quite intuitive and open, but that openness can cause issues in absorbing too much energy or being taken advantage of by others. HS men may strongly prefer to avoid confrontation, owing to the need to avoid overstimulation and simply to not have to think about the conflict for protracted periods of time. Setting effective boundaries is a process that is essential in a strong self-care practice for HS men.[49]

There are several considerations HS men should be aware of in establishing effective boundaries:

1. Discover your limits. This is only accomplished, unfortunately, by crossing a limit and discovering it to be the point at which you feel uncomfortable, angry, irritated, or hurt.
2. Be direct in letting others know when your boundaries are being crossed, preferably as nicely as you are able to, but more assertive if your boundaries are not respected. Learn to say no and mean it.
3. Allow for how your boundaries may make you feel. Know that you will have self-doubts about needing boundaries and that's the very reason that you need them all the more! Boundaries are there to keep you from being overstimulated, irritated, angry, or upset. Boundaries are there to protect you and allow you to avoid negatively stimulating interactions and environments, essential from a Vantage Sensitivity standpoint.
4. Raise your level of self-awareness. Often, we find a boundary is crossed because we have become complacent and allowed others to intrude further than they should have ever been allowed to, over time. Knowing how you are feeling is key to recognizing when you need to intervene before you become overstimulated.

5. Reevaluate your boundaries over time. You may find that they change as you become more self-aware or that some issues tend to lose their importance to you over time. If you find yourself feeling upset or uncomfortable with social interactions, it may be because your boundaries have slipped and need to be reset. We all change with time and age; therefore, you must adjust your boundaries as necessary.

In the same way that we deal with Misophonia, we also must be self-aware enough to interrupt the strong and quick emotions that accompany being highly sensitive. This doesn't mean that we are constantly in a state of hypervigilance, but it does mean that we have established appropriate boundaries beyond which we know will cause us to feel angry, upset, irritated, or exploited.

Some highly sensitive men may feel as if the idea of needing boundaries may make them appear feminine or weak, but our finely tuned nervous system does require special care! The good news is that once you have effective boundaries in place, you will feel much more confident in social interactions and in your ability to manage your life. As an integral component of your self-care practice elevate boundaries to prime importance.

Questions and answers

Does diet really matter? I hear all sorts of conflicting information.

Information does change over time as scientists learn more. However, there is a consensus that collectively, our sugar intake is far too high, we consume too many processed foods, and our carbohydrate intake is too high. Altogether, there is an epidemic of people being diagnosed with type 2 diabetes and if we wish to avoid that we have to modify our diets. The path to healing from disease is well-known: begin with diet.

I'm terrible at self-care because I'm so busy with work, family, etc. How can I fit in time?

We're all busier than our bodies were evolved to be, so we have to fit in self-care along the way. We can walk more, pay more attention to eating well, and ensure that we are getting adequate sleep. It may not be easy, but it is essential to care for our bodies.

Is it normal for me to sleep more than other people?

HSPs expend more energetically through processing all stimulation to a deeper degree. As an evolved survival strategy, SPS is expensive in terms of energy and time. Sleep is the way that we recharge, and it is not uncommon for all HSPs to sleep an hour or more than others do. This is totally normal.

Empowerment Points

- self-care is a necessity for HS men as their bodies expend more energy processing all stimulation.
- the right diet is the one that keeps your body in a state of well-being and does not encourage or support disease processes.
- reducing stress is about adapting your life to fit your unique needs.
- our sense of touch is connecting and one of the kindest things we can do for our partners. We are also deserving of touch from our partners.

- exercise is a key aspect of an overall self-care practice. Brisk walking is one of the easiest exercises you can do but choose an exercise that you will do consistently.
- sleep is a bedrock of mental health and stability. Prioritize your need for sleep! Highly sensitive bodies typically require more sleep than less sensitive people. Adapt your life so you are able to get the sleep you need to function well in life.
- setting boundaries is both a kindness for yourself and for others. Learn where your boundaries need to be set then set and enforce them! Reevaluate those limits over time and adjust as appropriate.

CHAPTER 9

Relationships

"The meeting of two personalities is like the contact of two chemical substances: if there is any reaction, both are transformed." ~Carl Jung

Men who are highly sensitive may find relationships to be one of the hardest areas of their lives to navigate as they contend with stereotypes regarding what people expect from men, the difficulty in finding the right partner, and living within a relationship as a highly sensitive man. Each of these areas presents complexities but it is possible to experience satisfying and fulfilling relationships with others as a HS man if one puts forth the effort to truly know oneself and commit to a lifelong inquiry into how to balance high empathy, strong, quick emotions, and deep internal thought processes. HS men are not for everyone but for those lucky enough to snag one, the rewards may be endless!

Cliches about men

It is an unfortunate fact of life for HS men that they must contend with dispelling stereotypes about what men are like that have been implanted in people's minds through culture, the mass media, and through perpetuation of mass mediocrity. Too often, women are guarded when meeting a new man and may expect for him to be more cliché than substance. For the HS man, this means he not only has to navigate a new relationship but must also overcome stereotypes about male behaviors that he may not even remotely identify with.

Few HS men would likely identify with being overly aggressive, sports-obsessed, dominant in all circumstances, or intolerant, yet men in general have an image problem in American society, perhaps worldwide, where the cliché of a man as a caricature is the image that pops into many people's minds. HS men, as well, may appear to be no different than any other man in terms of appearance or attire. Many HS men prefer to simply blend in with everyone else and not call any attention to themselves. While this may be good for reducing attention focused on the individual, it also lumps them in with everyone else and makes winnowing them out from the less sensitive men a challenge for potential partners.

Once a HS man feels comfortable in opening up to a potential partner, he may reveal enough to dispel any illusions about stereotypes. Gaining a HS man's trust and making him feel comfortable with you as a partner, even a friend, is step #1 in getting to know a HS man. With a sense of mutual trust, HS men, being highly empathetic, will likely sense that the new person is at least open to getting to know him and he will likely reciprocate in turn.

Highly sensitive men do especially well if in supportive, encouraging, and positive environments.[3] They do far less well if in negative, pessimistic, or abusive environments. Understand that a HS man may or may not have experienced a traumatic background. If he has, it is important to be patient with him and to allow him to reveal what he wishes to, in time. Never force a HS man because he will likely not respond the way you might like. HS men do not respond well to negativity in any form. You are dealing with a slightly different variation of a human who sees and thinks about the world in a slightly different way that embraces complexity, seeks real human connection, and is generally broader in range than in less sensitive men.

The HS man will enjoy going out but will also likely need to recharge in quiet. Bear in mind that all HS men, like all HSPs, are different from each other; no two are alike other than the core D.O.E.S. aspects of the trait. The HS man will enjoy deeper conversations but may also like downtime with little to no talking at all. HS men will, for the most part, be more introverted than extraverted but you will likely encounter about 30% who are extraverts. You will also find up to 50% to be high in sensation seeking, which is an entirely different trait that can complement but also complicate the overall psyche of the HS man.[51]

Befriending the HS man

If you would like to have a HS man as a friend, it's really not that hard. Simply be positive, don't push the relationship, and allow for the slightly different way he interacts with the world and needs to withdraw to recharge at times. In the end, he's not that different but he may be infinitely more nuanced, loyal, and have significant growth potential throughout life.

Many HS men will appreciate the small things that you do for them as friends. Being more sensitive to subtleties, HS men will appreciate the kind word, consistency, or the simple card! Remember, for HS men, meaning and connection are everything. You won't get far with them if you are superficial, untrustworthy, or manipulative. This does not sound anything like the cliché of the average man stereotype, right? It does not because the HS man is the opposite of the average man!

Befriending a HS man can easily lead to long-term friendships as he will tend to work to hang on to friends that he values. Many have been passed over as being too quiet, too nice (if you can believe that), or too out of step with the rest of the world. But it is precisely this difference that makes the HS man a man apart. If your intention is less than serious, please invest yourself in a less sensitive man. Highly sensitive men will do best with consistency in the friendship, lack of drama, and a reciprocal exchange of energies that enrich and transform both.

Finding the right partner

If you are a HS man, finding the right partner is familiar to you as a significant challenge in life. Do you consciously search for someone with particular qualities such as similar sensitivity or fairly common interests, or do you look for the exact opposite? In many cases, the concept of propinquity determines who we get to know and who we eventually choose to enter relationships with. Propinquity, or the social psychology notion that physical or psychological proximity between people is one of the key factors in determining attraction, reduces our pool of possible partners. HS men, who are more introverted – likely to be the majority – may have fewer choices, making the careful cultivation of their social circle all the more imperative. So, where do you go to meet people?

Highly sensitive men run the gamut of expressions of sensitivity and likely vary in their level of self-awareness. There are probably many more HS men who do not know they are highly sensitive than those who do. For those who came from supportive early environments and have evolved well throughout life, they have likely built very satisfying lives without any knowledge of being sensitive at all. This matters in that where one would go to meet people would likely vary as well based on levels of self-awareness of sensitivity and relative health of one's social network. This speaks again to propinquity and the people in our immediate physical and psychological spheres. Note that today people may find themselves interconnected psychologically with others who reside far from us and we are able to connect so easily through improvements in technology.

Online dating has boomed in recent years and one statistic from the Pew Research Center suggests that 30% of Americans report having used an online dating site.[76] There are advantages and disadvantages for the HS man to consider with online dating sites, let's begin with some of the advantages:

1. You control the pace at which things move.
2. You can meet many different types of potential partners.
3. You have time and space to think before responding to messages.
4. Possibility of meeting a partner from outside your immediate area.
5. It is a chance to practice meeting people, working on the social awkwardness of approaching others, and understanding how to conduct yourself in dating situations.
6. Potential partners you meet online may be the type of people you would never meet any other way.

7. If you are a high sensation seeker, online dating offers an endless variety of different experiences.

The advantages for HS men in using online dating sites to take their time in meeting others, to practice their dating cues, and to enlarge their pool of potential partners alters the dynamic to some degree but online dating can be a great way to build confidence in a fairly non-threatening way. There are, of course, some distinct disadvantages to the online dating world that HS men should be aware of:

1. People may lie completely or exaggerate one or more elements of their profile.
2. One must be very careful in meeting new people. Always meet in a public space.
3. Everyone on a dating site is there for a reason. Some are extremely picky, and few people meet up to their expectations, that's why they are there. There's every manner of strange person on dating sites!
4. Propinquity still factors in because the pool of local people is only so large.
5. People using dating sites may be simply "looking for fun" and nothing else.
6. It is easy to project an image online that may be harder to live up to in person. Always meet, at least via Skype, Facetime, or Zoom, before getting far into a new friendship. If they refuse or make excuses, bail out!

Whether you decide to venture into the world of online dating or not, it is one possible way to meet people that may or may not work for you. Should you tell others in your profile that you are a HS male? I suggest that you do not because to do so implies that you regard what is simply a marginally rare personality trait as a problem you have to tell people about upfront. SPS is not a problem; it's a simple genetic trait, we all have many traits and they are only one part of a larger picture of personality. A partner will learn about you if you spend time together and it will be obvious that you are not like other men, in very positive ways. Don't feel that you need to wear a sign that says "highly sensitive" on it; you aren't that different in the end.

There are many other ways to meet a partner. Many people still meet others through friends of friends, social groups, church attendance, and work. The important thing for you as a HS man is that you control the pace of how things proceed in a relationship because strong emotions can obviously overwhelm and cloud your judgement. Taking time to invest into a partner allows for the development of stronger, albeit slower, forms of love that are better suited to long-lasting relationships.

If you are a high sensation seeking HS man, your likely opportunities to meet people increase some because you are likely out and about more in search of novelty, new experiences, or thrills. HSS/HS men are very similar to HS men in that they have the core traits of SPS but also one or more of the four aspects of sensation seeking.[51] Meeting people for the HSS/HS man entails all of the same issues HS men face but with the complication of embodying two very different traits in many respects. It may be confusing for others to understand how you are able to be both sensitive and sensation seeking, since they do not seem, on the surface, to mesh well.

High sensation seeking HS men may be high in novelty and new experience seeking, known to also be a cross over for HSPs, making them seem to be more extraverted than they are. This may cause a partner to get a different first impression than will hold up later. In that sense, you may fit right in with other sensation seekers who are not HSPs, at least for a while until you need to withdraw and recharge on your own. Or until your high empathy, deep thinking and feeling, sensitivity to subtleties, and emotional range come into play. That's when confusion may set in for those who pegged you as merely another sensation seeker among many.

Sensation seeking is more accepted in many cultures and all people are sensation seekers to some extent.[77] Being high in sensation seeking will generally mean that you are high in novelty and new experience seeking and boredom susceptibility, the two big cross overs many HSPs seem to identify with. Meeting a partner may require that you really work to find someone who is capable of relating to your complexities. Sometimes that means another HSS/HSP! No one will understand your simultaneous needs for quiet and stimulation better than a fellow HSS/HSP. That commonality is, however, no guarantee that your partner's complexities as a fellow HSS/HSP will lead to a relationship.

Long-term life with a HS man

Long-term relationships are evolving entities throughout the life course. HS men, if they choose the right partner, meaning a partner who is kind, patient, understands that he needs his space, and is willing to grow along with him, may find the HS man to be the best of all catches!

Highly sensitive men may be wonderful partners and parents if there is a good dynamic in the relationship. HS men may be very conscientious and seek meaning through the people that they choose to invest themselves in. Raising children may be one of the most rewarding and fulfilling experiences of a HS man's life as there is a strong sense of purpose and responsibility, at least until the child grows up and becomes a young adult. The dynamic that exists between the partners in the relationship is an important one for HS men. Too often, HSPs generally suffer because they choose the wrong partner and stay in such a relationship far longer than they should. If the right partner is found, it is likely that the HS man will feel well-supported and positive about the present and future and will work to meet mutual goals and aspirations.

Sensitive Sexuality

The experience of sexuality for HS men is similar to other experiences where we must consider how the core D.O.E.S. aspects of SPS apply. The sensual part of touching a partner should be where HS men have an advantage but not if there is trauma or fear involved from the past. Some HS men may be quite cautious about sharing such an intimate experience with a partner, preferring to wait for that elusive perfect partner, whom they can trust implicitly. Others will feel differently and have close relationships that will provide experience with sexual technique and how to be with another person in an intimate setting.

The HS man as a lover could be quite a catch for the right partner! No two HS men are alike, but embodying the core aspects of SPS implies that the HS man may be:

- more attentive to the sexual desires and needs of his partner. As deeply conscientious people, HS men may bring that same level of focus and careful attention to lovemaking.
- Sensitivity to subtleties is an obvious plus for the HS male lover as he may be more aware of a partner's experience and, if he has some practice, be very good at timing and technique.
- High empathy may provide for a deeper, richer sexual experience for the HS man as he is able to almost feel the experience of his sexual partner. That level of connection should be very good for his partner as well.
- Overstimulation may be an issue, depending on the man. All HS men are different and will experience sex in a somewhat different way on a somatic basis. Some men may be overstimulated by certain sexual positions or acts and need to change to less stimulating ones. Others may enjoy the acting out of character and engaging in completely overstimulating, yet exhausting, sex.
- HS men may be quite creative as lovers if they choose to engage with it across their emotional range.

For the high sensation seeking highly sensitive man, the experience of sexuality may be significantly different as his main driver may be a need for new experiences and novelty, or thrill seeking. Sex is a perfect activity for physical thrill-seeking when you consider it. What can be more stimulating than sharing intimacy with a partner that puts you both in your optimal range of stimulation? HSS/HS men may be more daring and creative about their lovemaking but may also reach an exhaustion point from overstimulation and need to recharge. The sensitive side is never far from the sensation seeker and sex may be an area of life where the HSS/HS man throws caution to the wind and indulges his sexuality to the fullest.

Disinhibition obviously factors into the HSS/HS man as a lover. Where the HS man may feel inhibition and refrain from pushing his limits sexually beyond a boundary, the HSS/HS man may be quite disinhibited and explore his sexual boundaries to a greater degree. The trick for the HSS/HS man is to know when his need for sensation has been met and to not overdo it, for the sake of his partner, as well as to express his sexuality in a healthy way. It's important for the HSS/HS man to balance out his strong need for sensation-seeking by listening to that cautionary voice that will keep him balanced and level.

Questions and Answers

What is a good way to get to know a new person quickly?

One fun and interesting way might be to use social psychology researcher Arthur Aron's 36 questions. The questions are designed to share vulnerability and increase closeness between people through reciprocity. The questions are set up to become increasingly revealing. Begin with set 1 for 15 minutes then proceed to set 2 for 15 minutes and set 3 for 15 minutes. This ensures the same amount of time is spent at each level of disclosure.

You can find the 36 questions at https://ggia.berkeley.edu/practice/36_questions_for_incr easing_closeness.

Should I find a partner who is also an HSP? Wouldn't that be the best possible scenario?

Not necessarily, and I preface that by saying that, yes, it may seem preferable to share so much in common with a fellow HSP but bear in mind you will be with another HSP who has many of the same challenges as yourself, perhaps many more. Sometimes it can be better to be with a partner who is not highly sensitive at all because you can serve to counterbalance each other! Where one feels very strongly the other can inject timely rational thinking and objectivity or a comforting presence. Similarly, where one partner is uniquely attuned to other people the other partner may benefit if there is a lack of understanding about how to act in a supportive way. The opposite may also be true where a less sensitive partner has no clue at all about your experience of life and is completely ill-suited to your needs. You will need to experiment and meet a number of different personality types and not jump at the first one who smiles at you! What works for you in a partner will be highly specific and tailored to your needs, as well as vice versa. Kindness is one the biggest qualities you should seek in any partner.

I've tried the online dating sites and apps and dated in person but have never found the right person for a serious relationship. What's wrong with me?

There's nothing wrong with you because finding a partner is difficult for most people. HS men will spend more time overthinking their interactions and what they might have said, done, or done better; so much so that they drive themselves to distraction! If you're that hard on yourself consider what that is like for a new partner. Work on self-care first and building a life that has meaning and worth before bringing another person into it. It can be tempting to feel that we need a partner too early on in life, particularly for those of us who have been quite lonely throughout life, but it is still best to be secure in oneself and actively living a life that is balanced and works for you before including a partner. Likewise, sometimes when we are not even expecting it is when we will meet the perfect person.

Empowerment Points

- Culture has created an image of masculinity that others will expect to see you enact but you are not bound to fulfill these expectations. A potential partner should get to know the real you and not a role that you're playing that mirrors the cultural expectations.
- The best partner for a HS man is the one who can help provide and sustain a positive and supportive overall environment within the relationship.
- Highly sensitive men may be very good lovers and enjoy their sexuality tremendously with the right person.
- HSS/HS men need a partner who can understand and relate to both high sensitivity and high sensation seeking.

CHAPTER 10

Parenting

"If you are a parent, open doors to unknown directions to the child so he can explore. Don't make him afraid of the unknown, give him support." ~Osho

Becoming a parent can be a time of great anxiety for many HS men as they contemplate the early childhood environments they had and feel apprehension about either doing a better job than their parents did or upholding high standards of a supportive childhood. In this chapter, we will look at some of the most significant challenge areas and where the HS man may have a real advantage as a parent. Among the most relevant challenge areas are carrying over poor parenting practices learned from parents - if they were unsupportive or otherwise low-quality - managing sensitivities and need to recharge in a stimulating family environment and learning to cooperate with a partner to form a unified parenting strategy.

Not repeating the past

Highly sensitive men who experienced Adverse Childhood Experiences (ACEs) early in their lives may naturally feel some reticence about their ability to not repeat the same mistakes that led to their ACEs. This fear feeds directly into the core aspects of SPS to process all experiences in a more elaborate way in the mind to glean the lessons from the past. HS men are, in some important ways, better equipped to notice when their behaviors are repeating familiar patterns. They notice subtleties and may pick up on their own telltale signs of parenting in a way they would prefer not to before it becomes an issue. In a sense, HS men may be self-policing parents who own their actions and seek to do the best job they are capable of as deeply conscientious people.

Highly sensitive men with ACEs in their backgrounds may also feel a lingering sense of emptiness or lack of wholeness, as if there is a missing segment of one's being that continually calls out to be satisfied in some way. This missing piece phenomena can fuel anxiety, low-level lifelong depression, and an undercurrent of anger that is mystifying to the individual. HS men who suffer in this way have a responsibility to themselves to heal but also to their children, so they do not allow new damages to be inflicted upon old damages.

The good news is HS men may make terrific fathers! Our natural conscientiousness coupled with our high empathy and caring demeanors are perfect for raising children. Likewise, if we came from an unsupportive background, we know what that looks like and will take steps to avoid becoming a possible self we do not wish to be. That's a strong motivator of behavior!

Managing sensitivities as a parent

Many HSPs seem to express the idea that being a parent would be too overstimulating, but most parents learn to prioritize and manage all stimulation. HS men vary in how self-aware they are, what their overstimulation triggers are, and how they recharge. A reasonably self-aware HS man would be best equipped to be a parent in that he would fully understand what it means to be highly sensitive and will have adapted his life before becoming a parent. One of the most significant sources of stress for many parents is career and HS men who have worked out how to have the right career, meaning a career that truly works for them, will encounter less stress on a daily basis and have more energy for his children.

Knowing the types of stimulation that tend to overwhelm us is very important as we will often be tasked with doing things with our kids that we might not do otherwise, like helping with their sports teams or school activities. Understanding that at times we will be overstimulated by activities is part of being a parent and we learn to develop patience, grace, and to turn the focus away from our inner processes and onto our kids. Often, by removing the focus from our sensitivities and being hyper aware of them, we learn to lessen our threshold for overstimulation. I'm not suggesting that this is exposure therapy, but it is something similar and learning to lessen our sensitivities to some degree will pay benefits across the spectrum of activities we engage in throughout life.

There are a few things to keep in mind with overstimulation as boundary points:

- Know how you're feeling emotionally at any moment and know when to step back and take a few moments to gather yourself. Good communication with your partner will help in these moments.
- It's okay to be overstimulated at times and not to feel guilty because you are. Every parent gets overstimulated by their kids at one point or another; it happens.
- Your children will notice over time how you tend to cope with overstimulation. The way you cope is likely how and what you will teach them. You have

to decide, do you show an inability to cope or strength through patience and perseverance?

If you have not worked out how to be in public spaces that may be noisy at times, being in such spaces will force you to consider your coping mechanisms and develop de-stressing techniques that work for you. Kids, in that sense, can be the greatest incentive we may have to not accept limitations. Rest assured that when you are the dad that your kids look to for strength and guidance you will find it inside of yourself!

Cooperating with parenting partners

One of the most important jobs HS men have is to provide a supportive and nurturing early environment for their children. Many HS men have experienced the opposite of support in their own childhoods and may be fearful of making mistakes that will cause problems for their children, especially boys. It's easy to overthink our every action as a parent, but the good news is that we can relax because the parenting load is not all on our shoulders. We do have partners in parenting in the form of our spouses, parents, extended relatives, and community. Take advantage of those partners to lessen some of the stress and allow you to focus on the big stuff like keeping a sustainable household structure and routine in place. Focus on loving your children and investing your time in them. Don't worry too much about not doing it exactly right because there is no absolute in parenting. If anything, show up for your children as a whole adult who they can count on and look up to for guidance and support.

It is easy for HS men to become overprotective of their children as they apply the conscientiousness HSPs are known for to parenting. Children can be lovable bundles of joy that we want to protect at all costs, but it is critical to allow them to explore and learn from doing. In our world of easy distractions enabled by technology it is all the more imperative that our children be outdoors and be allowed to indulge themselves in ways they enjoy. Obviously, be mindful of their safety but don't overthink it or project your fears onto them too much. As long as the environment is a reasonable place to feel safe in and there is supervision, your kids will likely be perfectly fine!

Ten tips for being a good parent

1) Be the parent you wanted. Most of us, even those who had good childhoods and great parents, want to change some things about how we embody parenthood. Be kind with your children, be patient as they express emotions, and be loving. Allow your kids to watch how you conduct yourself and be aware that they are imitating your behaviors. Being the parent that you wanted can be terribly rewarding but also challenging as you will need to invent it as you go.

2) Be consistent and firm but kind. Children depend on you to be consistent in your rules and enforce those rules and will push you to find weaknesses they can exploit. A consistent structure works best for highly sensitive children because they know what to expect and will feel more secure if navigating the world rather than anxious or fearful. Kindness will smooth over the firmness.

3) Be a safe haven. Kids need to know that parents are their safe haven where they will always be loved

unconditionally. Such kids grow up to have a firm foundation to build on later in life.

4) Talk it over. Sit with your children and let them talk about their thoughts, feelings, and experiences. That's how they will make sense of it all and make connections in the brain. Help them to learn to think rationally by teaching them critical creative thinking at a young age.

5) Practice self-care. Don't forget to keep yourself healthy and balanced so you are able to show up for your children in a rested and steady state. As a role model, you are setting the tone. Your bad habits may become their bad habits, but the opposite may also hold true. Teach your children to calm themselves through focusing on their breathing and to be self-aware of how they function.

6) Keep your mission in mind. It's all too easy to lose sight of what we're doing as parents as we face the crush of responsibilities but bear in mind that your job is finite and focused on raising your children to become happy, healthy, productive, ethical adults. There will be periods where it all seems endless but, eventually, your children will be grown and off on their own.

Being a Dad is one of the greatest roles you can play in this lifetime. It will force you to grow in ways you may have never thought possible, but you will find it within yourself to become more of an adult than you ever dreamed to be possible. Being a dad entails a necessary vulnerability and openness with your children, indeed, with many children. That may or may not come naturally for you as a HS man, but you will learn in time, and it will become second nature as you get to be a few years into it.

Let them build!

More than simply not being too overprotective, allow your kids to build things and learn to use their creativity and their hands! Teach them how to design things out on paper and how to make that design a reality. Start with something simple like a birdhouse where you can teach them measuring, cutting, and fastening methods. Then, proceed to bigger and better projects. I remember a time when I wished to build things but had no support from my dad. Later in life, I decided I had to indulge that need to build and constructed my first log cabin out of cedar trees that I cut myself. I built an outdoor shed not long after, then what would become my largest project to date: an 800 square foot story and a half log cabin!

I had to teach myself all of the skills that my dad might have taught me. We did work on one project together in 1976, a small shed in our backyard and perhaps that whetted my appetite to do more, and I will always remember that project. I would have loved to have built more things with him as I grew into a teen, but the fact that he passed way at just 49 meant building would have to wait.

If you were like me, teaching your kids to build will also allow you to heal some of the lack of Dad-time you had with your own father. Few things in life are better than watching your own children acquire and use a skill that you taught them! The ulterior motive behind teaching kids to build is that it also builds self-confidence and self-esteem.   Your kids might even have their first flow experience!

Building and creating things is an all-inclusive process of learning by doing, by engaging with concepts and applying them directly. What may seem abstract on a blackboard is clear when one needs a board cut to a very specific length or width. The skills involved in building are transferable to all aspects of life as the confidence and sense of accomplishment can cross-pollinate other new projects and problems. Yes, your HS boy might pop his finger with a hammer, but he will only do that once! With power tools, obviously supervise their use and train your HS child how to use them safely and properly. Withhold use of larger power tools like a table saw, chop saw, or chain saw until your child is about 15 or so (do those cuts for them).   Jig saws, drills, scroll saws, band saws, hammers, nails, screws, glue, paint, stain, and most other items used in building should be safe, but read the directions and follow them for safe use. Set the tone on safety and it will last them a lifetime.

Questions and answers

How can I keep from becoming too overstimulated with noisy children in the household?

This is a problem for any HSP but one way to mitigate noise is to have them play outside as much as possible. Noise tends to dissipate outdoors and the feeling of being cooped up is alleviated to a degree by being outside. Knowing your boundaries for overstimulation are obviously important as a parent, particularly with newborns and infants. The first two years can be quite trying for any parents and HS men should plan to share equally in all child-rearing activities. Being there for your partner or spouse will help you develop patience and grace about what it takes to be a parent. Being a parent is challenging in many ways, but also extremely rewarding and fulfilling. You should not necessarily avoid becoming a parent because you fear overstimulation. You will adapt.

How do I know if my child is a highly sensitive person?

There's no way to know for sure but babies who are fussy or who cry a lot may be demonstrating a greater sensitivity to the stimuli in the environment. Once a child is a bit older the core D.O.E.S. aspects may begin to present themselves to some extent. If you think your child might be highly sensitive, it's important to be more patient as a parent with him and to provide a positive, supportive environment but to not stigmatize or overprotect him.

My spouse is not an HSP, but I am, how do we manage to negotiate the challenges of parenting?

You can be most effective as a parenting couple through consistency in your behaviors and expectations with your children, being supportive of each other, and by being patient with the ups and downs that will inevitably come with parenting. Parenting is the greatest job you will ever have but is definitely not easy.

Empowerment Points

- If you had an unsupportive childhood, you will likely not repeat that same behavior with your own children. In fact, HS men may make terrific fathers.

- Your self-care practice is essential as a parent but make it such that you can teach your children how to practice good self-care as well.
- You are not alone in parenting. Your partner or spouse is equally invested in providing care for your children. Don't assume all of the responsibility and be willing to share it with extended family if they wish to help.
- Being a good parent is synonymous with being a good person overall; the difference is, with children you are their role model.
- Let your kids get their hands dirty and build things! They need to learn to work with their heads, hearts, and hands.
- Life is tough! Kids will get into dust ups with other kids, crash their bikes, and get extremely dirty. Allow all of it because they will learn to be assertive, resilient, and exercise grit.

CHAPTER 11
Empowering the Sensitive Male Soul

Throughout this book we have looked at a number of important areas of life that are salient to the HS man. We have examined the nature of culture and masculinity, while emphasizing that each of us has a part to play in enacting masculinity in the way we feel most authentic in. We have unpacked the complexities of career and explored key issues in ways that add to our thinking of career as an externalization of our already rich inner worlds. We have discussed the toll that being highly sensitive takes on our bodies and minds. Self-care has become our mantra that enables us to maintain a balanced approach between what the world asks of us and how we may arrange our lives to fulfill those needs while doing so in a personally sustainable way.

The problem of anger has found articulation and tied us back in with self-care as we explored the importance of emotional intelligence and boundaries. Creativity and viewing our lives as creative processes ever-unfolding has become part of our lexicon and added to our overall strategy for how we might live our lives. The crucial areas of relationships and parenting have been explored, emphasizing the importance of finding the right fit with a partner and the development of confidence as a parent.

All of these areas demonstrate that the path for HS men is one of gradually coming to a greater awareness of and appreciation for their trait. Empowerment comes through being able to confidently embody our traits in the world and use them for productive, positive ends. Before we can fully embody the true gifts of the trait, we need to grow our capacities and nurture them over time. There is no substitute for investing in ourselves!

Invest in Yourself!

Highly sensitive men vary just as much as grains of sand, but we are united in that we all seem to be concerned and engaged in the inner work of healing from wounds throughout life, realizing our innate potential, and finding wholeness. Carl Jung said we may spend our entire lives simply trying to be whole and complete persons and never make it to focusing on pursuing self-perfection. Some of us may be more successful in some ways than other HS men, while others are well on their path to wholeness. There are a few major points to consider with investing in ourselves:

- Every investment we make in ourselves will help lead us to wholeness over time but may also improve our quality of life in the present.
- HS men are of sufficient psychological complexity as to need significant mentoring and coaching to make realizations along the way.
- Our path is always irrevocably tied to our need for a positive, supportive environment.

It is only through a willingness to invest in ourselves that we may reap the rewards that come with soul-searching, introspection, and reflection along with positive actions. The philosopher Alan Watts taught us that it is folly to seek some realization of a higher self because we always end right back where we started because we're already whole and complete, we just don't know it or have forgotten. The investments we choose to make in ourselves may only serve to empower us in ways that allow us to function better in the world with greater ease and purpose, but we are, in essence, filling a bucket that is already full.

The trick to investing in ourselves is to invest in others as much as for ourselves because it is through our relationships that we truly come into our own. Many HS men are introverted and may be happily absorbed in their own minds and inner worlds of meaning and context but applying that same focus outwardly onto others spreads the wealth and enriches the lives of others as we serve as mentors, coaches, role models, and wise sages. Our role as sensitive members of society has never been a traditional one, it has always been as the ones who realize things before others do, who see the implications and consequences, and for whom daily life carries with it a richer possibility that demands that we blaze and follow our own paths.

That path will never be quick or easy. Life is not a proposition of getting through it with as little inconvenience as possible. It is, rather, acknowledging that our human nature is irrational and often self-serving. Struggling with our own sloth, our own dishonesty about who we are, and using that darkness to realize our fundamental humanness as imperfect beings living an improbable existence on a planet that is, as far as we know, possibly the only place in this universe with such life, should enliven us as manifestations of the cosmic creative force experiencing itself through our eyes to push it as far as we are able. There is a fitting German word for this notion: sehnsucht, meaning a wistful longing for alternative states in life even if they are imperfect and unattainable.

What you can do to help your HS Man

If you are the spouse or partner of a HS man, you have a truly special human being in your midst. Your HS man may seem quite different than men you have known in the past and it will take longer to get to know and appreciate the HS man's gifts and capacities, but once you do, you will realize that he is unlimited in his potential and only needs a supportive and positive environment in which to grow and flourish.

Your HS man may have experienced trauma, conflict, abuse, or neglect in his past and will be slower to trust you but once you gain his trust, he will be loyal beyond belief. He is a deeply conscientious man who needs for things to be done well and for life to move at his pace. He will never fit well with the traditional model of masculinity or believe that he should. You can best support your HS man by allowing for who he is at heart and accepting his tremendous potentiality.

Your HS man will have stronger emotions than many men you may have known, and he may be quick to laugh or cry, but he will possess an immense inner strength rooted in an intense experience of life. He will likely notice the spring flowers before others, connect easily with animals and children, and feel the pain of others. He will likely react at times with great irritation or anger and be quite off-putting. He may also, at times, feel like it is all too much, and he needs to shut himself away and recharge. Allow him that time and space so he can come back refreshed and ready to think about meaningful endeavors in life, how to help others grow and develop, or simply to experience the sublime beauty and irony in life.

If your HS man is also a high sensation seeker, the story is only somewhat different. Your HSS/HS man will need novelty and new experiences to stay engaged in life and will flounder without them. The HSS/HS man will be susceptible to boredom and will continually need to reinvent himself throughout life. With the HSS/HS man you will not find that he will be the type who ever be truly "settled." The HSS/HS man will always be restless to some degree and on the cusp of the next thing. He will be endlessly interesting because he will dive deep into fascinations and accumulate vast depth and breadth of knowledge and experiences, but he will also be deeply reflective and in search of meaning and context.

With the HSS/HS man you can best help him by not trying to remake him in a lesser image. It may help for the HSS/HS man to have a partner who is more solid and grounded and who can attend to some of the long-term details like financial planning and maintaining some semblance of daily routine so you both have a structure to accomplish things within. If anything, the HSS/HS man may be so interested in each new thing that he misses the point about patience and sticking to a current goal. Rest assured that once he learns the value of achieving goals, he may be incredibly focused and achieve great things.

Combining high sensitivity with high sensation seeking is an extraordinary combination in one person where depth meets sheer exuberance and wonder. Your HSS/HS man may be, above all else, intensely curious about many things and complex in disposition and affect. He may be intrinsically creative as he has both a deep mind, notices subtleties, and is encouraged to pursue interesting directions through the dopamine "hits" he gets in the brain's pleasure pathway when he encounters novelty. The HSS/HS man's need to reinvent, to give meaning to life, and to express his strong empathy and intuition in ways that feel authentic to him will keep you intrigued but also will require your patience and loving support.

The Quiet Leaders: Why we so Desperately Need you to Step up

The world seems to have an overabundance of "noisy" leaders, those who have no qualms about loudly bulling their way through people, places, and things to get what they want. Many are deeply egocentric and sociocentric individuals and follow their own selfish agendas, while caring little for the growth and development of those who help them achieve their goals. In fact, many of these leaders are not very effective leaders at all when it comes to motivating people intrinsically because they rely entirely on fear, volume, and intimidation. The quiet leader, by contrast, subtlety manipulates people to help them realize their common goals, while providing opportunities along the way for people to grow and become leaders themselves.

A quiet leader is the true leader who understands and values people. He works from a place of altruism not ego and tends to eschew accolades in favor of recognizing the team that made it happen. The quiet leader is intellectually humble, probably gifted, and will accumulate and employ greater social capital. That social capital will be earned through careful relationship building so the quiet leader has a network of skilled and willing talent to call upon when he needs it. The quiet leader is most likely to have the brilliant new ideas and to institute the culture-changing paradigm shifts, for example, Martin Luther King. When the quiet leader decides to speak, he can truly command attention.

The workplace of the 21st century is now, and is more diverse, more complex, and requires more finesse than for leaders of previous generations. The quiet leader is desperately needed at all levels of society to make things work the way we need them to while growing the capacities and capabilities of the next generation. The quiet leader is YOU if you choose to accept the role. If this all seems aspirational, that's because it is and you will need to work towards building yourself into the quiet leader in your workplace, your social groups, or in your communities.

The problems facing the world are complex, mired in competing interests, and wicked, grand scale problems that will require leaders with vision, creative thinking meshed with critical thinking, and the ability to bring others along as he progresses. The quiet leader is uniquely suited, by virtue of his disposition, to address these issues and wield the levers of power in a benevolent way that empowers others. Power is nothing if it not used well.

Wabi Sabi

The Japanese aesthetic concept of Wabi Sabi seems a fitting way to summarize the experience of the HS man. Wabi Sabi is twofold: wabi is imperfection, irregular beauty, austere in expression and form, and serenity, while always changing and is never quite attainable. Sabi is treasuring the weathering effects of time that naturally degrade and consume all things in the natural cycle of life and death. Wabi Sabi together is a way of viewing life that appreciates simplicity, fragility and that celebrates the broken parts.

Western culture prizes and privileges perfection, permanence, and symmetry. Wabi Sabi reveals the subtle beauties in fragility, impermanence, and asymmetry. I cannot think of a better metaphor for the lives of HS men than Wabi Sabi in that on our paths to individuation we confront and embrace our broken parts. Japanese culture has a concept called *kintsugi* whereby they repair cracks in pottery by sealing them with lacquer and dusting the repair with gold powder. In effect, kintsugi celebrates the broken parts and raises them to conscious attention where they can then be observed and appreciated.

To realize our wholeness, we must see the cracks that have appeared throughout our lives and learn from them because they represent where we have disintegrated and been reborn, time and time again. If we fill those cracks with gold, we celebrate our own imperfection, fragility, and impermanence. Thinking of our lives as ever-unfolding creative processes that bend and break at times keeps us humble, grounded, and focused on the growth and joy we can experience in the here and now. Western culture largely seeks to place metaphorical carrots in front of our noses and entice us to work just "a few more years" or just "a little harder" to get the carrot, which, many times, never comes. Wabi Sabi, by contrast is unadorned, simple, and pregnant with meaning in the true now.

The lives of HS men are the pottery shards that have buckled and broken numerous times over a lifetime as he finds his way along an uncertain path that only he can travel. Coming to an appreciation of our imperfect, uncertain, and finite paths through this life leads us to a greater love and respect for the present moment.

Empowering the sensitive male soul

This book has sought to cover many of the most relevant and significant areas of life pertinent to HS men and to do so in a way that has not been written about before. As we draw this book to a conclusion, we are left to consider what it means to empower a person? To empower someone, doesn't it mean that they were not empowered before? If so, in what ways were they not empowered? Highly sensitive men may or may not fit the categories of empowered or not empowered as we are all different and have had different life trajectories. Indeed, many HS men do well with their creative, helping dispositions, ability to note subtleties, high empathy, and ability to connect on deep levels with others. We may also do quite well as hard science thinkers and explorers who can put to use our rich talent for invention, logic, and conscientiousness.

Other HS men have experienced setbacks early in life that have colored their view of the world as an unwelcoming and frightful place where one would do well to simply "get by" without too much change or disruption in routines that keep them stable and feeling relatively secure. Yet others, particularly HSS/HS men have found life to be a constantly evolving and unfolding entity that they are always on the cusp of but never quite in control of. Empowerment for all of these various groups of HS men implies that we are primarily engaged in a consciousness raising activity whereby we encourage and support HS men of all types in their emotional, spiritual, and intellectual growth and development.

Empowerment implies that we equip HS men to understand their trait better and then teach them how to embody it in ways that uniquely work for them. Each HS man's situation and circumstances will be dissimilar, and we can only provide the means with which they may increase their understandings of masculinity and help put them on a path to greater self-awareness, awareness of SPS, and impress upon them how none of us are truly alone as HS men.

Highly sensitive men hold tremendous potential to change the world through our often-high intelligence, our divergent and convergent thinking, and due to many of us feeling rejected by society. Creatives that feel a sense of rejection may take that as a sign to simply dig in deeper and develop their interests and passions to levels they might not have otherwise – consider Vincent Van Gogh, for instance. Throughout history, HS men have made some of the greatest scientific discoveries and pushed society forward. It takes a unique individual who is decidedly different in special ways to even consider that there might be alternative approaches to a problem. The inventor Nikolai Tesla, for example, has had far-reaching implications that are playing out today. There's even a company named after him! Sir Isaac Newton, as well, approached scientific inquiry from a completely different angle than less sensitive persons might have. Albert Einstein, most recently, is an exemplar of productivity in solitude, strong intuition, visual thinking, and a keen sensitivity to the world.

The aim of this book is not to promote the idea that HS men are damaged or suffering from a pathology that needs to be fixed. Rather, it is an acknowledgement of the often-high potential inherent in these men and a clarion call to us to empower them to achieve their full potential. The issue of masculinity and hegemony is a powerful one but, as we have said, SPS tends to moderate the effects of culture and HS men need to invest in developing and growing their capacities and talents regardless of culture.

Far from accepting narrow definitions of what it means to be a man in today's world, as communicated by society, we HS men are freer than ever to fully employ our high empathy, our broad emotional and psychological range, and our deep minds in service to higher goals and aspirations for all people, if we choose. For the HS man who suffered numerous ACEs in childhood, and there are far too many of us, heal yourself and don't allow limitations to define who you are or what you can be in this life. For the HS man who has done well enough in the world yet felt that sensitivity is more of a burden than a gift, find ways to realize the potentiality of high empathy, sensitivity, and your kind heart. For the HS man who has pushed through it all to significant degrees of personal and career success, reach out to those who are still on the climb and offer a hand up. Your sensitive brothers need to know you are there, that you have made it, and that they can too.

Life may feel like a solitary journey at times, but it is through connecting with others that we know who we are, that we recognize our fundamental humanness; that we are not so very different in the end as human beings walking the same path towards the truly meaningful and worthwhile higher goals in life. We all come from various families at different levels of society, but we are all united in our experience of sensitivity as a defining aspect of our lives and together, we will rise.

About the Author

Tracy Cooper, Ph.D. is a high sensation seeking highly sensitive man, an assistant professor at Baker University teaching in the Ed.D. in Leadership and Higher Education program, a researcher and author of several books: Thrive: The Highly Sensitive Person and Career, Thrill: The High Sensation Seeking Highly Sensitive Person, and numerous podcasts, interviews, and articles. He most recently co-founded an annual highly sensitive men's weekend with Elaine Aron, Ph.D. and John Hughes. His website may be found at drtracycooper.org, on Facebook @tracycooperphd, LinkedIn at tracycooperphd, and Instagram at tracycooperphd. He lives in the Springfield, Missouri area with his wife, Lisa and one doting female Siamese cat.

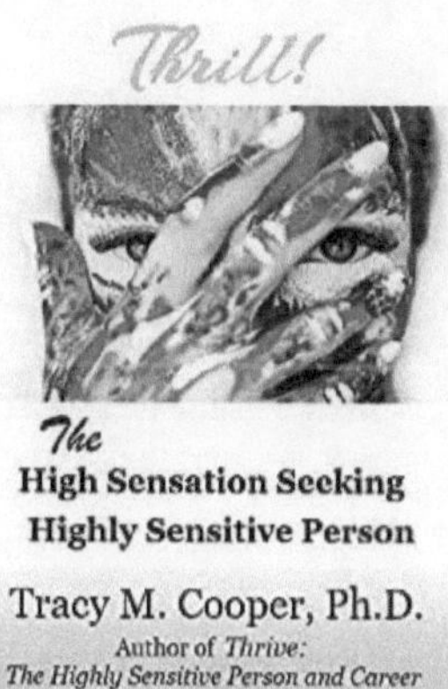

Endnotes

[1] Aron, A., & Aron, E. (1997). Sensory-processing sensitivity and its relation to introversion and emotionality. *Journal of Personality and Social Psychology, 73,* 345-368.

[2] Belsky, J. & Pluess, M. (2009). Beyond diathesis stress: Differential susceptibility to environmental influences. *Psychological Bulletin,* 135, 885–908.

[3] Pluess, M., & Belsky, J. (2012, October 1). Vantage Sensitivity: Individual Differences in Response to Positive Experiences. Psychological Bulletin. Advance online publication. doi:10.1037/a0030196

[4] Acevedo, B., Aron, A., Aron, E., Sangster, M., Collins, N., & Brown, L. (2014). The highly sensitive brain: An fMRI study of sensory processing sensitivity and response to others' emotions. *Brain and Behavior, 4,* 1-15.

[5] Acevedo B, Aron E, Pospos S, Jessen D. (2018), Review: The functional highly sensitive brain: a review of the brain circuits underlying sensory processing sensitivity and seemingly related disorders. *Philosophical Transactions,* B 373: 20170161.

[6] Buss, D. (1999) Human nature and individual differences: The evolution of human personality. As cited in Handbook of Personality: Theory and Research, Pervin and John.

[7] Assary, E., Zavos, H., Krapohl, E., Keers, R., Pluess, M. (2020). Genetic architecture of environmental sensitivity reflects multiple heritable components: a twin study with adolescents. (n.p.).

[8] Chen, C., Chen, Chuansheng, Moyzis, R., Stern, H., Qinghua, H., Li, H., Zhu, B., & Dong, Q. (2011). Contributions of dopamine-related genes and environmental factors to highly sensitive personality: A multi-step neuronal system-level approach. PLOS ONE, 6, 1-9.

[9] Licht, C, Mortensen, E, Knudsen, G. Association between Sensory Processing Sensitivity and the 5-HTTLPR Short/Short Genotype. Center for integrated molecular brain imaging.

10 Zuckerman, M. (1994). Behavioral expressions and biosocial bases of sensation seeking. Cambridge University Press.

11 Zuckerman, M. (2007). Sensation seeking and risky behavior. American Psychological Association. Washington, DC.

12 Kimmel, M. S. (1994). Masculinity as homophobia. In H. Brod & M. Kaufman (Eds.), *Theorizing masculinities* (pp. 119–141). Thousand Oaks, CA Sage

13 Kimmel, M. S. (2006). *Manhood in America: A cultural history*. New York, NY: Oxford University Press.

14 Lee, R. B., & Daly, R. (1999). *The Cambridge encyclopedia of hunters and gatherers*. Cambridge, UK: Cambridge University Press.

15 Murdock, G. (1934). *Kinship and social behavior among the haida*. American Anthropologist.

16 Christian, D. (2008). *Big history: The Big Bang, life on Earth, and the rise of humanity* [audiotape]. San Diego State University Lecture Series.
Chantilly, VA: Teaching Company.

17 Stearns, P. N. (2007). *A brief history of the world*. George Mason University Lecture Series. Chantilly, VA: Teaching Company.

18 Zeram, J. (2007). *Patriarchy, civilization and the origins of gender*. Retrieved from the Anarchist Library website:
http://theanarchistlibrary.org/HTML/John_Zerzan__Patriarchy__Civilization__And_The_Origins_Of_Gender.html

19 Daileader, P. (2001). *The Early Middle Ages* [audiotape]. College of William and Mary Lecture Series. Chantilly, VA: Teaching Company.

20 Daileader, P. (2004). *The High Middle Ages* [audiotape]. College of William and Mary Lecture Series. Chantilly, VA: Teaching Company.

21 Seidler, V. J. (1994). *Unreasonable men: Masculinity and social theory*. New York, NY: Routledge.

[22] Kimmel, M. S. (1987). Rethinking masculinity: New directions in research. In M. S. Kimmel (Ed.), *Changing men: New directions in research on men and masculinity* (pp. 74-93). Newbury Park, CA: Sage.

[23] Kimmel, M. S. (2008). *The gendered society* (3rd ed.). New York, NY: Oxford University Press.

[24] Rotundo, E. A. (1993). *American manhood.* New York, NY: Basic Books.

[25] Brannon, R., & David, D. S. (1976). *The forty nine percent majority.* New York, NY: Random House.

[26] Chapman, D., Whitefield, C., Felitti, V., Dube, S., Edwards, V., and Anda, R. (2004). *Adverse childhood experiences and the risk of depressive disorders in adulthood.* Journal of Affective Disorders. P. 217-225.

[27] Aron, E., Aron, A., & Davies, K. (2005). Adult shyness: The interaction of temperamental sensitivity and an adverse childhood environment. *Personality and Social Psychology Bulletin, 31,* 181-197.

[28] Pluss, M., and Belsky, J. (2013). *Vantage sensitivity: Individual differences in response to positive experiences.* Psychological Bulletin: Vol. 139, 4, 901-916

[29] Whitehead, S. W. (2002). *Men and masculinities.* Malden, MA: Blackwell.

[30] Henslin, J. (2013). *"Essential of sociology."* New York, NY: Pearson.

[31] Zeff, T. (2010). *The strong sensitive boy.* San Ramon, CA: Prana Publishing.

[32] Jung, C. (1921). *Psychological types.* Collected Works, Vol. 6. Princeton, NJ: The Princeton University Press.

[33] Ghiglieri, M. P. (1999). *The dark side of man: Tracing the origins of male violence.* Cambridge, MA: Perseus.

[34] Aron, A., Aron., E., & Jagiellowicz, J. (2012). Sensory processing sensitivity: A review in the light of the evolution of biological responsivity. *Personality and Social Psychology Review, 16*, 262-282.

[35] A. Khaleque, R. P. Rohner. Transnational Relations Between Perceived Parental Acceptance and Personality Dispositions of Children and Adults: A Meta-Analytic Review. *Personality and Social Psychology Review*, 2011; 16 (2): 103 DOI: 10.1177/1088868311418986

[36] Vasquez, R. (2019). What role do women play in toxic masculinity? Wisconsin Public Radio, January 25. Retrieved from https://www.wpr.org/what-role-do-women-play-toxic-masculinity

[37] Morin, E. (1999). Homeland Earth. Hampton Press, Inc. Cresskill, NJ

[38] Aron, E. (2010). Psychotherapy and the highly sensitive person: Improving outcomes for that minority of people who are the majority of clients. New York, NY: Routledge.

[39] Sampson, R. (2002). Bullying in schools. Guide No. 12. https://popcenter.asu.edu/content/bullying-schools-0

[40] Mendaglio, S. (2008). Dabrowski's theory of positive disintegration: A personality theory for the 21st century. In Mendaglio, S. (Ed.) Dabrowski's theory of positive disintegration, Great Potential Press.

[41] Piechowski, M. (2008). Discovering Dabrowski's theory. In Mendaglio, S. (Ed.) Dabrowski's theory of positive disintegration, Great Potential Press.

[42] Mika, E. (2008). Dabrowski's views on authentic mental health. In Mendaglio, S. (Ed.) Dabrowski's theory of positive disintegration. Great Potential Press

[43] Dąbrowski, K. & Piechowski, M. M. (with Marlene Rankel and Dexter R. Amend). (1996). Multilevelness of emotional and instinctive functions. Part 2: Types and Levels of Development. Lublin, Poland: Towarzystwo Naukowe Katolickiego Uniwersytetu Lubelskiego.

[44] Dąbrowski, K. (1972). Psychoneurosis is not an illness. London: Gryf Publications.

[45] Cooper, T. (2015). Thrive: The highly sensitive person and career. Invictus Publishing, llc. Ozark, MO

[46] Jaeger, B. (2004). Making work work for the highly sensitive person. New York, NY: McGraw-Hill.

[47] Brod, H., & Kaufman M. (Ed.). (1994). *Theorizing masculinities.* Thousand Oaks, CA: Sage.

[48] Brannon, R., & David, D. S. (1976). *The forty nine percent majority.* New York, NY: Random House.

[49] Falkenstein, T. (2019). *The highly sensitive man: Finding strength in sensitivity.* Kensington Publishing Corp., New York, NY

[50] Vansteenkiste, M., Ryan, R. M., Soenens, B. (2020) Basic psychological need theory: Advancements, critical themes, and future directions. Motivation and Emotion, 44 ,1-31

[51] Cooper, T. (2016) *Thrill: the high sensation seeking highly sensitive person.* Invictus Publishing, llc, Ozark MO

[52] Greenleaf, Robert K. *The Servant as Leader.* Robert K. Greenleaf Center, 1991.

[53] Kinsey, Sharon B. B. "Quiet Leadership: How to Create Positive Change without the Noise and Negativity." *Journal of Extension*, vol. 48, no. 5, 2010, pp. 1–4.

[55] Ingram, Osmond C. Jr. "Servant Leadership as a Leadership Model." *Journal of Management Science and Business Intelligence*, vol. 1, no. 1, Oct. 2016, pp. 21–26., doi:https://doi.org/10.5281/zenodo.376752.

[56] Sousa, Milton, and Dirk van Dierendonck. "Servant Leadership and the Effect of the Interaction Between Humility, Action, and Hierarchical Power on Follower Engagement." Journal of Business Ethics, vol. 141, no. 1, 2017, pp. 13–25.

57 Bloom, N., & Roberts, J. (2015). "A working from home experiment shows high performers like it better." Retrieved from https://hbr.org/2015/01/a-working-from-home-experiment-shows-high-performers-like-it-better.

58 Kaufmann, S. (2016). Myth of the alpha male. https://archive.org/details/podcast_ta-talk-sex_the-myth-alpha-male-w_1000368975602

59 Seligman, M. (2006). Learned optimism: How to change your mind and your life. New York, NY: Random House.

60 Aron, E. (2010). Psychotherapy and the highly sensitive person: Improving outcomes for that minority of people who are the majority of clients. New York, NY: Routledge.

61 Hendriksen, E. (2018). *How To be yourself: Quiet your inner critic and rise above.* St Martin's Press. New York, NY.

62 Csikszentmihalyi, M. (2008). Flow: The psychology of optimal experience. HarperCollins. New York, NY.

63 Paul, R. & Elder, L. (2014). Critical thinking: Tools for taking charge of your professional and personal life. Pearson Education, Upper Saddle River, NJ

64 Brout, J. J., Edelstein, M., Erfanian, M., Mannino, M., Miller, L. J., Rouw, R., Kumar, S., & Rosenthal, M. Z. (2018). Investigating Misophonia: A Review of the Empirical Literature, Clinical Implications, and a Research Agenda. *Frontiers in neuroscience, 12,* 36. https://doi.org/10.3389/fnins.2018.00036

65 Cavanna, A. E., & Seri, S. (2015). Misophonia: current perspectives. *Neuropsychiatric disease and treatment, 11,* 2117–2123. https://doi.org/10.2147/NDT.S81438

66 Jastreboff, P., Jastreboff, M. (2014). Treatments for decreased sound tolerance: Hyperacusis and misophonia. Seminars in Hearing, 35, 2.

[67] Seeman, T. E. (2000). Health Promoting Effects of Friends and Family on Health Outcomes in Older Adults. *American Journal of Health Promotion, 14*(6), 362–370. https://doi.org/10.4278/0890-1171-14.6.362

[68] Horney, K. (1991). Neurosis and human growth: The struggle towards self-realization. W.W. Norton and Company, New York, NY

[69] Jung, C. (1921). *Psychological types.* Collected Works, Vol. 6. Princeton, NJ: The Princeton University Press.

[70] Montuori, A. (2008). The joy of inquiry. Journal of Transformative Education,6, 1.

[71] Paul, R., & Elder, L. (2008). The thinker's guide to the nature and functions of critical and creative thinking. Foundation for Critical Thinking Press. Sonoma, CA.

[72] Csikszentmihalyi, M. (1992a). Flow: The psychology of happiness. London: Harper and Row.

[73] Ludwig, D. S., Hu, F. B., Tappy, L., & Brand-Miller, J. (2018). Dietary carbohydrates: role of quality and quantity in chronic disease. *BMJ (Clinical research ed.), 361,* k2340. https://doi.org/10.1136/bmj.k2340

[74] Goldstein, P., Weissman-Fogel, I., Dumas, G., Shamay-Tsoory, S. (2018). Brain-to-brain coupling during handholding is associated with pain reduction. Proceedings of the National Academy of Sciences Mar 2018, 115 (11) E2528-E2537; DOI: 10.1073/pnas.1703643115

[75] McGonigal, K. (2019). The joy of movement: How exercise helps us find happiness, hope, connection, and courage. Avery, Penguin Random House.

[76] Vogels, E. (2020). 10 facts about Americans and online dating. Pew Research center. https://www.pewresearch.org/fact-tank/2020/02/06/10-facts-about-americans-and-online-dating/

[77] Zuckerman, M. (1994). Behavioral expressions and biosocial bases of sensation seeking. Cambridge University Press.

9 798632 782876